FROM DETENTE TO ENTENTE

Q. Is NATO now redundant? If it is what would u put in its place. + if it is not what role would be played by either the EC or the CSCE in the new Eur.

BRASSEY'S ATLANTIC COMMENTARIES

Atlantic Commentaries present a series of introductory surveys of important issues affecting the Atlantic Alliance and its future. The booklets are written and edited with the general reader as well as the specialist in mind and are intended to provide insights into a number of different aspects of East–West and intra-Alliance relations. Among future topics planned are Spain's evolving role in European and transatlantic affairs; the role of NATO in the wider world; global security; and the interdependence of European, Japanese and United States security interests. Other subjects to be covered will include regional security issues, political and economic topics, country studies and future perspectives for international stability in the changing political environment of the 1990s.

Brassey's Atlantic Commentaries are produced in association with the NATO Information Service and various national Atlantic Committees or other associations and institutions concerned with different aspects of security. The opinions expressed are the responsibility of the editors and the contributors and do not necessarily represent the official views of NATO or of individual governments.

Brassey's Atlantic Commentaries

NATO's Defence of the North
Eric Grove

The Western European Union and NATO
Alfred Cahen

NATO 2000
Jamie Shea

Titles of related interest from Brassey's

DROWN
A Single European Arms Industry?

GROVE and WINDASS
The Crucible of Peace: Common Security in Europe

HANNING
NATO: Our Guarantee of Peace

RIES
Cold Will: The Defence of Finland

RIES and SKORVE
Investigating Kola

SLOAN
NATO in the 1990s

Heads of State and Government at the London Summit, 5–6 July 1990. (NATO Information Service)

BRASSEY'S ATLANTIC COMMENTARIES No. 4

FROM DETENTE TO ENTENTE

*An Alliance in Transformation
A Greater Europe in Creation*

MARK EYSKENS
Minister of Foreign Affairs of Belgium

Edited by NICHOLAS SHERWEN and FREDDIE JOCHMANS

BRASSEY'S (UK)
(Member of the Maxwell Pergamon Publishing Corporation)
LONDON · OXFORD · WASHINGTON · NEW YORK · BEIJING
FRANKFURT · SÃO PAULO · SYDNEY · TOKYO · TORONTO

UK (Editorial)	Brassey's (UK) Ltd., 50 Fetter Lane, London EC4A 1AA, England
(Orders, all except North America)	Brassey's (UK) Ltd., Headington Hill Hall, Oxford OX3 0BW, England
USA (Editorial)	Brassey's (US) Inc., 8000 Westpark Drive, Fourth Floor, McLean, Virginia 22102, USA
(Orders, North America)	Brassey's (US) Inc., Front and Brown Streets, Riverside, New Jersey 08075, USA Tel (toll free): 800 257 5755
PEOPLE'S REPUBLIC OF CHINA	Pergamon Press, Room 4037, Qianmen Hotel, Beijing, People's Republic of China
FEDERAL REPUBLIC OF GERMANY	Pergamon Press GmbH, Hammerweg 6, D-6242 Kronberg, Federal Republic of Germany
BRAZIL	Pergamon Editora Ltda, Rua Eça de Queiros, 346, CEP 04011, Paraiso, São Paulo, Brazil
AUSTRALIA	Brassey's Australia Pty Ltd., PO Box 544, Potts Point, NSW 2011, Australia
JAPAN	Pergamon Press, 5th Floor, Matsuoka Central Building, 1-7-1 Nishishinjuku, Shinjuku-ku, Tokyo 160, Japan
CANADA	Pergamon Press Canada Ltd., Suite No. 271, 253 College Street, Toronto, Ontario, Canada M5T 1R5

Copyright © 1990 Brassey's (UK)

All Rights Reserved. No part of this publication may be reproduced, stored in a retrieval system or transmitted in any form or by any means: electronic, electrostatic, magnetic tape, mechanical, photocopying, recording or otherwise, without permission in writing from the publishers.

First edition 1990
Library of Congress Cataloging-in-Publication Data
Eyskens, Mark.
From detente to entente: an alliance in transformation: a greater Europe in creation/Mark Eyskens: edited by Nicholas Sherwen and Freddie Jochmans.—1st ed.
p. cm.—(Brassey's Atlantic commentaries; no. 4)
1. Europe—Politics and government—1945– 2. World politics—1985–1995. I. Sherwen, Nicholas.
II. Jochmans, Freddie. III. Title. IV. Series.
D1053.E97 1990 327'.09'04—dc20 90-46767
British Library Cataloguing in Publication Data
Eyskens, Mark
From detente to entente: an alliance in transformation: a greater Europe in creation.—(Brassey's Atlantic commentaries series)
1. Military alliances
I. Title II. Sherwen, Nicholas III. Jochmans, Freddie
355.031
ISBN 0-08-040731-5

Printed in Great Britain by BPCC Wheatons Ltd, Exeter

Contents

ABOUT THE AUTHOR vii

EDITORIAL INTRODUCTION ix

Chapter 1 **The Implosion of Communism** 1

Chapter 2 **The Necessity of European Union** 46

Appendix 1 The Belgian Memorandum of 20 March 1990 60

Appendix 2 The London Declaration on a Transformed North Atlantic Alliance (6 July 1990) 69

INDEX 75

MARK EYSKENS

About The Author

ECONOMIST, historian, member of the Belgian House of Representatives, former Minister of Development Co-operation, Minister of Finance, Prime Minister, Minister of Economic Affairs and now Minister of Foreign Affairs, painter and distinguished academic, Mark Eyskens has played a leading role in the many national and international councils of which he has been a member.

Born in April 1933, in the university town of Louvain, where he still lives, he acquired his first degree when he was twenty, was adviser to the Minister of Finance before he was thirty, and went on to combine a remarkable academic career with close involvement in national and international political life. He assumed ministerial rank at the age of 43 and has since played a key role in successive Belgian governments under Prime Ministers Tindemans and Martens in particular, and as Prime Minister himself from April to December 1981. He has been a member or chairman of numerous boards and associations as well as a Governor of the IMF and of the World Bank. Honoured in many different countries, he holds distinctions in scientific and other fields and has published extensively in Dutch and in French.

As Foreign Minister of a country which has been a founder member of virtually every one of the transatlantic and European institutions created since the Second World War, Mark Eyskens might be forgiven for thinking that he is currently involved in non-stop roadshow. While other members of the cast may sometimes rotate, Belgium is present at almost every scene—routine ministerial meetings and special summits, NATO, EC, WEU, the Council of Europe and back to NATO. With bilateral meetings and informal contacts in addition to the schedule of multinational discussions, often addressing different aspects of the same basic agenda—European integration, developments in Eastern Europe, German unification, Western security, the transatlantic partnership—Ministers of Foreign Affairs need a clear mind as well as stamina. Mark Eyskens has both, in large measure. At the same time he brings to his writing an intellectual energy and depth of perceptive analysis which command close attention.

The reader of *From Detente to Entente* may take issue with some of its arguments but would be rash to dismiss them lightly, for, like earlier famous Belgian contributors to the European political process, such as Paul-Henri Spaak and Pierre Harmel, Mr Eyskens combines practical political experience with the kind of vision that is once again required to shape Europe's destiny in the modern world.

Editorial Introduction

SUCH is the complexity of the discussion of future European security structures and the dynamic of change in East–West relations that students of today's history can no longer afford to take a narrow view. The broad distinction between bilateral and multilateral diplomacy remains, but it is no longer possible to examine in isolation individual institutional arrangements for addressing issues of concern to Europe and its transatlantic partners. The concept of security includes economic progress and stability. Economic development cannot be assured without regard for the security of the environment on which it depends. He who wishes to explore the prospects for the development of European union must therefore be aware of the opportunities and constraints affecting the realignment of Europe's internal and external political relationships. The European Community cannot operate without taking into account security concerns any more than the North Atlantic Alliance can ignore developments within the Community.

The explosion of change in the Soviet Union and the nations of Central and Eastern Europe, and in their relations with other countries, has in fact thrown open doors between neighbouring but formally separate structures in the West in no uncertain terms. When all constants have become variables, it is no longer possible to deal in compartmentalised notions of defence, foreign policy, economic development, social progress and environmental concerns, each with their separate and independent mechanisms for co-ordination at the international level. They are all interrelated.

In this *Atlantic Commentary* Mark Eyskens brings together not only the concepts of Europe's security and economic identities, both with their inherently political implications, but also, implicitly, the much less precise notions of the European and Atlantic communities. Each of these has, at times, been guilty of encouraging too narrow a definition of their scope. The Atlantic Community has remained, essentially, a useful concept which enables the transatlantic partnership between the European members of the North Atlantic Alliance and their North American allies to be explained in terms of historical, cultural and ethnic links, shared risks and common values. The European Community is the formal title adopted by the core of twelve European countries which have created common institutions and are moving forward towards economic and monetary union as well as an ever closer political relationship. It has more precisely defined attributions than the Atlantic Community but both of them are increasingly seen as associations which must reach out to their neighbours, not as exclusive clubs reserved for their members. In the light of the opening up of Central and Eastern Europe, lingering doubts over that important distinction are being overtaken by events. While the formal expansion of European Community membership from twelve to fourteen or more countries may not be on the immediate agenda, the role of the EC is increasingly becoming that of an agent for stability and progress in Europe with which many countries who are not currently signatories of its treaties can be closely associated. The Atlantic Alliance is seen more and more as a successful agency for peace which can now embrace the legitimate security interests of the whole of Europe. No geographical extension of its formal role is implied now any more than in the past. Consultations within the Alliance are not subject to any limitations and encompass developments outside the area defined in Articles 5 and 6 of the North Atlantic Treaty as a matter of course.

This growing interdependence and indivisibility is not foreseen in the literature which has grown up round the institutions of the Alliance and the European Community themselves. Once the basic machinery for managing the inter-European, East–West and transatlantic relationships in the post-war years had been created, the points of reference for studying those relationships remained relatively static. The temperature of international relations, particularly across the East–West divide, went up and down. The diplomatic successes and failures of the various institutions—NATO, the OECD, the EC, the Council of Europe, the WEU, EFTA,—could be charted and analysed, but the overall picture remained obscure. What, after all, could be the common ground between, for example, an organisation on one continent with some degree of centralised decision-making authority, created to manage economic development in an expanding internal market of twelve nations; and one with decision-making possible only by consent from sixteen sovereign centres of authority, designed to provide a political and military security structure spanning two continents across an ocean? The European Community had one role, NATO another. The other institutions occupied similarly water-tight compartments. Distinct roles meant little dialogue and even less interaction. There were common meeting points, such as the Helsinki process, the North–South dialogue and ad hoc arrangements to deal with out-of-area threats or economic aid for Eastern Europe. However, there were too many active disincentives for any form of rational co-ordination and effective interaction—not least the absence of key member countries from some of the forums. The pattern was one of invisible threads binding together a few common goals rather than a coherent design. Policy-making in many of the centres of decision was the art of the gymnast, able to balance short-term interests and expediency, not that of the choreographer with an awareness of the overall, longer-term effect. The trick was to work within separate spheres whose membership in some cases overlapped but whose identities were essentially distinct. It is these spheres, like bubbles, which are now colliding and merging—if not structurally then at least in conceptual terms. And new spheres have appeared or are planned: the Group of 24, the Conference on Security and Co-operation in Europe (CSCE), and so on.

It is worth pausing to consider why this development is taking place. The answer is not hard to discover. Recovering from the trauma of World War II, healing the scars it had inflicted on friend and foe, and living with the artificial East–West division which came in its wake—these were enough to concentrate the mind wonderfully on building up a web of internal ties while containing external threats and risks wherever they could be identified. The time to develop historic opportunities had not yet come. Mistakes could be made—and there were plenty of them—without the need for more than a minor adjustment of the calendar. 'Europe' could be limited to six member countries until expansion became possible; a European defence community could be created but if it failed to materialise, no matter, other means would be found. There were moves afoot to create an Atlantic Community, but without real substance it remained at the level of ideas. And there were recurrent bouts of nervousness about supranationalism which also slowed down the pace. Situations might come close to disaster but crises could be managed and no price-tag could be attached in either case, since history had yet to issue its real challenge.

Since 1989 the course of international events has taken a different turn. Today's developments make the planner's task far more complex as well as enriching the field in which he works. Functional demarcation lines continue between the various forums set up to co-ordinate policy at the international level, but European and transatlantic relations, economic progress, political stability, scientific advance and environmental conservation are all now subjects which have a direct bearing on each other and which affect all our nations by the course they take. Dropping out is not an option.

Mark Eyskens brings to the study of all these issues a historian's perception of the role of the past in shaping the conditions of the future. He has an intuitive sense of the temporary and the permanent in the ebb and flow of internationalism and is determined to focus on the permanent. He identifies the real issues confronting the Western political and economic systems in the aftermath of the implosion of the communist system and sees them as components of a single problem requiring a co-ordinated set of solutions. Any reader inclined to dismiss the need for such an approach as a pipe-dream for utopians will be left in no doubt that the question in Mr Eyskens mind is not whether unified, coherent thinking can be achieved, but whether any other approach is affordable. Mr Eyskens believes not, and he has no hesitation in saying so.

The basis for this study was written in January 1990 and was first published in booklet form by the Belgian Ministry of Foreign Affairs. The text was substantially revised by the author in April 1990 to take account of more recent events. Trying to keep abreast of the tide of international political change has become an author's and a publisher's nightmare—like trying to keep a meal hot for guests who arrive late.

The Editors make no apology for not inviting Mr Eyskens to put his dish back in the oven yet again. They are convinced that there is more than enough food for thought here which will remain fresh and tempting for many months to come. Some of his proposals will not be implemented. Others have already taken on considerably more concrete form and now offer a realistic glimpse of the future. But if there is one aspect of this essay which should not be overlooked, it is that the dynamic of co-operative, non-confrontational politics now underway does not allow time for the reactive responses of the old order. Nor will it accommodate any hedging of bets. The convergence of national and international interests has ceased to be a far-off goal. It is a day-to-day reality, the recognition of which has become the key to progress. The historic opportunity which is so often held aloft as the banner of the nineties is nevertheless not on offer unconditionally. Europe must fulfil its destiny but its transatlantic dimension must be preserved and reinforced. East–West confrontation must be relegated to the history books but East–West co-operation can only be constructed on the basis of mutual respect for legitimate security interests and guaranteed stability. Stability is in fact the condition which allows purposeful change to be accommodated.

It will take considerable skill to manage the current transitional period without accident. Today's political leaders are nevertheless fully aware that they are making tomorrow's history and that can only be a good thing. Mark Eyskens is one of those who needs no lessons in this respect. Underlying his reasoned argument is the conviction that opportunities, historical or otherwise, seldom make a second appearance. We are, he says, 'being driven by events' and if that is true, we had best know where we are going.

1. The Implosion of Communism

A Structural Break With History

The events of 1989 in Central and Eastern Europe illustrate—sometimes dramatically—the bankruptcy of a regime, a system and an ideology: communism.

The history of the 20th century has been characterised by the rise and fall of two great totalitarian systems: Fascism-Nazism and Communism. The first large-scale practical application of Marxism started with the October Revolution of 1917 in Russia. At the end of this century, 72 years later, the dominant impression is that the communist experiment, based on Marxism-Leninism, has failed; this parenthesis in history is now coming to a close. But the victory of democracy over totalitarianism, of freedom over dictatorship, has exacted an unimaginably high price in human terms, one that can be quantified in tens of millions of lives.

One day, the history of the 20th century in Europe will be seen to have been marked by these pivotal events which changed the course of history.

Since the end of World War II, there has been no war in Europe. Europe has known the longest period of peace in its millennia-long turbulent history. It is true that the Cold War raged between the Eastern and Western Blocs. Keeping each at bay from the other by a strategy of mutual deterrence that included the threat of a nuclear war.

The total absence of war in Europe seems in itself to point to a far-reaching shift in European history. Conventional weapons have never proved an adequate deterrent to conflict. The outbreak of the

Signing of the Rome Treaties

First and Second World Wars demonstrates this. Since 1945 and the entry on the scene of the atomic weapon with its apocalyptic dimension however, it seems that a fundamental change has taken place in the strategy of the rival blocs, provided that their leaders continue to behave rationally.

A second break with history occured when, shortly after World War II, a start was made in Western Europe on European Unity in the form of the ECSC[1] and the EEC[2]. European integration marks a major break in European history. For more than 2000 years, the countries of Europe have been constantly at war with one another. This has never

---

[1] European Coal and Steel Community. Established under the Treaty of Paris on 18 April 1951 by Belgium, France, Italy, Luxembourg, the Netherlands and the Federal Republic of Germany.
[2] European Economic Community established on 25 March 1957 under the Treaty of Rome.

been truer than over the past 150 years, with Germany and France cast in the role of arch-enemies. European integration appears to have established among the countries of Western Europe a *Pax Europeana*.

It is especially since the coming to power of Mikhail Gorbachev in the Soviet Union in 1985, however, that we can speak of a true change of direction in history.

Gorbachev's policy reduces essentially to five major initiatives:

With *glasnost* the Kremlin is attempting to restore the great political freedoms: freedom of expression, of assembly, of movement, etc. *Glasnost* paves the way for respect for human rights and an end to the Gulag Archipelago.

Perestroika is aimed at boosting the efficiency of the Soviet economy by the introduction of free market forces. This means the dismantling of central planning, granting a large degree of autonomy to business enterprise, the reintroduction of private initiative and of private property, the abolition of state monopolies, the acceptance of the profit motive as an economic force, etc. It is evident that, with *perestroika*, Marxist-Leninist doctrine has been disavowed on a number of essential points.

On many occasions, Gorbachev has reaffirmed his renunciation of the Brezhnev doctrine, whereby the Soviet Union was entitled to intervene in the internal affairs of countries within its zone of influence, for the purpose of defending international communism and promoting it worldwide, and was entitled to prevent these countries—by military force if necessary—from going their own way politically (Berlin 1953, Hungary 1956, Prague 1968 and Jaruzelski's military coup in Poland in 1981 are all examples of the doctrine in action).

The renunciation of this policy marks a fundamental change of course in Soviet foreign policy and has made possible the political evolution now taking place in Czechoslovakia, Poland, Hungary, the GDR, Bulgaria and Romania. Breaking with the Brezhnev doctrine also means breaking with Leninism and with the philosophy calling for the worldwide expansion of communism. At the same time, it has meant the undoing of post-World War II realities that were endorsed at Yalta.

The nationality problem within the Soviet Union is nothing more than a sort of process of decolonisation similar to the one which

Western countries lived through 20 or 30 years ago. Gorbachev is attempting to solve this problem by opting for a far-reaching confederation, with greater internal autonomy conferred upon the republics that make up the Soviet Union. Maintaining the political monopoly of the Communist Party seems here to be primarily an instrument to preserve national unity.

Finally, there is the disarmament which the Soviet leadership has been forced to adopt under the pressure of the economic collapse that is partly the consequence of the enormous Soviet armaments expenditures (15–20 per cent of GNP) in recent years.

Gorbachev's policy is literally 'revolutionary' because it offers the prospect of an end to the Cold War, the prospect of the so-called 'satellite' countries being able to liberate themselves from Soviet domination and go their own way, a greater chance for democratisation, and the prospect that communism—or what remains of it—is going to renounce a number of the essential credos of Marxism-Leninism such as class warfare, the dictatorship of the proletariat, the panacea of central planning, the ultimate world triumph of communism, the leading role of the Communist Party, the collectivisation of production resources, the satisfaction of human wants according to need and not according to merit.

The causes of the implosion of communism

The tremendous difficulties with which communism is confronted, both as an ideology and as a political system, are attributable to the increasingly apparent contradictions of Marxism-Leninism. Marxism and many Marxist thinkers have for decades analysed *ad nauseam* the contradictions of capitalism—such as the inherent self-destructiveness of competition. Thus, Marxists have never ceased predicting the inevitable and imminent collapse of capitalism.

But that is not what has happened. Capitalism has evolved into a mixed economic system under which high economic growth has made it possible to build an extensive system of social security. Per capita real income in the countries of the West has risen sixfold since 1914—an absolute historical record. In spite of all attempts by Nikita Khrushchev and others, the Soviet economy has not succeeded in catching up with that of the United States, nor that of Western countries generally. On the contrary, it has fallen ever further behind. In the meantime, Japan and certain South East Asian countries have taken advantage of the market economy to achieve extraordinary results.

According to Marxist doctrine, the dictatorship of the proletariat during a transitional phase is inevitable. But, this transitional phase has lasted since 1917, so it is difficult for the Soviet ideologists to hold out as credible the promise of the imminent dawning of true communism in the third phase of the dialectical evolution of history.

Communism has not brought equality—quite the contrary. The net gap in income between the highest and the lowest salaries is greater in the Soviet Union than in Western countries. To compound matters further, rationing and the harshness of the corruption and privilege of the *nomenklatura* have combined to render the inequalities of communism even more shocking. The abuses perpetrated by certain leaders, which are now coming to light, reinforce the impression that a 'people's democracy' can easily degenerate into a true kleptocracy.

In the time of Karl Marx, labour and capital were the key elements of production. Today, the major element of production is knowledge. Knowledge structured and channeled by computer. At the same time, research and development (R&D) are essential for technological and economic progress. The key factor in economic production is human creativity.

Creativity in turn requires imagination and a critical sense. Knowledge does not readily lend itself to the Marxist recipe of collectivisation and nationalisation of the means of production, unless the aim is to immerse the entire community in a climate of mental obscurantism. But such irrationality soon takes its toll and leads to technological and economic stagnation. The emergence of knowledge as the key factor in economic production could not be foreseen by Karl Marx in the 19th century. We have here a structural mutation that has confronted Marxism with an insurmountable ideological obstacle.

Marxist doctrine predicted increasingly destructive colonial and imperialist wars among capitalist countries. This is not what happened. The Western countries have, *bon gré mal gré*, granted independence to their colonies, and peace has reigned among the nations of the West for 45 years.

Increasingly, the market economy has shown its superiority over a planned economy; even in social terms, the market economy has produced remarkable results through remedial measures to insure adequate redistribution. The communist countries are now being obliged, under the pressure of circumstances, to adopt elements of the market economy. For orthodox Marxists, this is real heresy which is irreconcilable with the old beliefs.

Leninism placed great importance on the 'universal mission' of communism, and on the need to proselytise worldwide. The crushing of the popular uprising in Hungary in 1956 and of the Prague Spring in 1968 under the Brezhnev doctrine certainly did not lead to economic and social progress—quite the contrary.

Another major factor has been Soviet expansionism, particularly under Stalin, which, after the Second World War, imposed communist dictatorship on the countries of Eastern Europe, and led to growing antagonism between the two superpowers. These events, in turn, led to the unleashing of an arms race the cost of which, particularly for the Soviet Union, has now been shown to have become unbearable.

According to Marxism, history is determined by living conditions, by production resources and by class warfare waged by the masses. The fact that one man, Mikhail Gorbachev, has been able to bring about such radical changes, since his appointment as leader of the Kremlin, provides abundant proof of the impact of certain individuals on the course of history. In the eyes of an orthodox Marxist, Gorbachev is a living paradox and a contradiction.

There are serious and growing dissensions within the Communist Party of the Soviet Union—of which the discussion about the Party monopoly is but one aspect—which are contributing to the destabilisation of the communist system in the fatherland of communism. Certain policies advanced by Gorbachev are explicitly anti-communist and even anti-socialist and must shock and distress orthodox Marxist-Leninists. Those who are well off under the Soviet régime are apprehensive of *perestroika* and are afraid that they may see their privileges disappear.

Opening of the first McDonald's restaurant in Moscow.

Nor are the members of the military who, as a result of ever more stern disarmament measures, must prepare themselves for a difficult period of retraining for civilian activity, very enthusiastic supporters of Gorbachev's policies. And then, there is the entire Russian people which is aware that the new policy of the Soviet leaders is not yielding concrete results in terms of their standard of living. The dogmatists, the conservatives, the malcontents, the members of the *Nomenklatura*, and the reformists who have become increasingly impatient with the slowness of *perestroika*—all form a common front that, on the domestic scene, poses a serious threat for Gorbachev's political survival. To that is added the highly explosive nationalities problem.

The technology of dictatorship

We have been stunned by the lightning changes in the countries of Central and Eastern Europe, the absolute whirlwind of reforms, the rapid collapse of the Communist Party's monopoly of power, the overthrow of the iron dictatorship of Ceausescu in Romania. Still more amazing, however, is the fact that the communist dictatorship has persisted in all these countries for almost 45 years.

The explanation for this is obvious. Communism was introduced into these countries by the Soviet Union, with the active support of the Soviet Army, which behaved at the time as a conquering power and an army of occupation.

In addition, the technology of dictatorship, the spider's web woven by the state security complex, and by the propaganda apparatus of the media, assumed Orwellian proportions and contributed greatly to maintaining the communist régimes.

Doubtless, there was also such a thing as a communist ideal which exercised a strong influence shortly after the Second World War on intellectuals and on influential individuals who, especially in Central and Eastern Europe, had been severely traumatised by the inhuman practices of the Nazi régime. And in postwar Western Europe, too, particularly in the Latin countries, strong communist parties developed which applauded the régimes in the Eastern Bloc, while leftist intellectuals, from 1945 until about 1975, were deeply influenced by Marxist and neo-Marxist doctrine. Raymond Aron termed this phenomenon 'the opium of the intellectuals'.

Even more incredible is the fact that communism has been able to survive in the Soviet Union since 1917. This is doubtless attributable to a number of specific factors. Russia has never known true democracy. The short period of the Kerensky Government in 1917 is certainly not representative. For the average Russian, the transition from the absolute monarchy of the Tsars to Stalinism was not all that different. Even under the Tsars, there existed the secret police, concentration camps, and exile to Siberia. Moreover, the Russian Revolution was able to count on popular support and gain credibility by its promises to put an end to the feudal excesses of the Tsarist régime and to the flagrant social injustices. In a country still predominantly agricultural, that had barely emerged into the first phase of industrialisation, the centrally planned economy also seemed the most appropriate means of transforming the newly-founded Soviet Union into a modern industrial power. And the Communist Party seemed to be the ideal cement to consolidate the Union of Soviet Socialist Republics. The courage and bravery of the Soviet Army and of the Russian people in their struggle against the invading Nazi forces contributed substantially after the war, to the régime's prestige, particularly when it was learned that the Soviet Union had become an atomic power, and that its technological progress had put it in a position to play a pioneer role in the conquest of space (the first space satellite, named 'Sputnik' was launched in October 1957).

The attraction of the West and of Europe

The implosion of the communist régimes was largely caused by a series of internal factors, and the most important of these have been described earlier. But there are also a number of external elements which undermined the very foundations of the communist system.

The Conference on Security and Co-operation in Europe, Helsinki, 1975.

Foremost among these was the growing success of the Western European model of society, amply highlighted by the progress toward European unification and integration. The revolution in information and in the media meant that the countries of the Soviet empire could no longer be kept in mental isolation. By what could be termed the 'law of comparative advantages', the balance was tipped very strongly against communism.

The building of the Berlin Wall and the violent suppression of the popular uprisings and the movements for democracy in Hungary and Czechoslovakia were to have dire consequences for communism. These events also dealt a fatal blow to communist parties in Western Europe.

The movement in Western countries for respect of human rights was given powerful political support by the Helsinki Agreements and the so-called Helsinki process (particularly by the 'Basket III' of the Helsinki Final Act). It can now safely be said, in retrospect, that the Conference for Security and Co-operation in Europe was imperceptibly boring little holes in the Berlin Wall and so ensuring its sudden collapse.

Developing and maintaining a joint NATO strategy despite numerous obstacles, exerted increasing pressure on the Soviet Union and on the other countries of the Warsaw Pact, and confronted the Eastern Bloc countries with a very clear dilemma: either enter into an economically destructive arms race, or agree to negotiate on disarmament and détente. The Harmel doctrine with its shrewdly thought-out dual track: creating a credible defence deterrent on the one hand, and systematically exploring the opportunities for détente and disarmament negotiations on the other, forced the Warsaw Pact countries onto the defensive, especially when it appeared that this NATO policy was being pursued despite the anti-nuclear protests in Western Europe.

It was primarily the economic successes of the Western World, however, and the growing gap in living standards between the citizens of the Free World and those of the Eastern Bloc, that increasingly opened the eyes and heightened the malaise of those in the East. The serious economic crisis that hit Western economies, starting in 1975, failed to stem the tide in the countries of the Eastern Bloc. The proponents of the convergence theory who, at the end of the Second

World War, advanced the view that capitalism and communism would gradually grow toward one another and their differences gradually vanish, were proved completely wrong. Through all these years, the Western model of society has exercised an increasing attraction—at times bordering on fascination.

No excessive self-satisfaction

It would, however, be rash and irresponsible for the West to adopt a triumphalist attitude. Articles such as those by Francis Fukuyama[3] in which it is stated that the West has won the Cold War and that the dramatic successes of the Western model of society put an end to all ideological debate, overstate the case and are dangerous, since they can lead to crippling self-satisfaction.

In any event, the Western democracies are also faced with enormous challenges. Although the Third Industrial Revolution may explain the implosion of communism, it also presents our Western democracies with very serious challenges.

First of all there are the strains between technocracy and democracy which themselves entail a danger for democratic decision-making. Monopolies of knowledge can endanger democracy. This also applies to an excess of information, which leads to disinformation whereby public opinion, no longer able to grasp the complexities, becomes indifferent to politics. There emerges a sort of 'law of diminishing knowledge' and its corollary, the fact that more and more individuals are reaching the limits of their intelligence in a society which places an ever higher price on intelligence. In addition, firms that are in the vanguard of technological innovation, often achieve dramatically declining costs: this easily leads to impairment in the operation of competitive market forces and to the excessive concentration of power.

The market economy is constantly threatened by the formation of monopolies and cartels. It is only the market economy based on competition that offers the benefits held out by economic theory. An authority is required—preferably a supernational one—to keep the

---

[3] Francis Fukuyama, The End of History: The National Interest (Washington DC Summer 1989).

market economy ever mindful of the rules by which the game is played. Moreover, the market economy does not solve all problems: protection of the environment, redistribution of income in favour of the less fortunate, full employment, the major technical and social projects—all of these require judicious government intervention. Disproportionate emphasis on economic determinism leads to a mechanistic view of the economy, to the application of Newton's Law to the economic process and ultimately can lead to oppression of the individual.

The comments above highlight only one aspect of the increasing complexity of modern society, including the Western pluralistic democracies. That complexity confronts the individual with new forms of alienation that differ markedly from those described by the Marxists and the neo-Marxists. The individual becomes one cog in a vast machine: he becomes immersed in anonymity: the structures of society deprive him of his personality. He feels himself powerless, left to the mercy of blind forces he does not understand and over which he has no influence. We are living in an era of the anonymous and the impersonal. The citizen at the end of the 20th century is an object of dehumanisation. This dehumanisation is both social and existential. It is social by virtue of the increasing complexity of the structures of society: it is existential because the popularisation of scientific knowledge of the nature of the universe has destroyed the sense of the wonder of being and reduced the mystery of being to a temporary 'backlog' of still unsolved problems. Man thus feels himself a misfit in society and an orphan of God.

In the absence of an ideology to hold on to, certain forms of narrow nationalism are once more rearing their heads. This also applies to racism and to all manifestations of intolerance, fed by the demagogy of the neo-fascist parties. Increasing internationalism and the concomitant acculturation can evoke violent reactions that increase the strains in our society to an intensity that is sometimes dangerous.

Another factor is the demographic decline in the West. In the near future, one third of the population will be over the age of fifty, with all the consequences this implies not only for the funding of retirement benefits but also for the predominant outlook of the society. It is neither the Greens, nor the Reds, nor the Browns that will dominate the political scene—but the Greys.

The protection of the environment will probably become the most urgent problem. Twenty years ago, it was hardly discussed and even less so a century ago, at the time of the great ideological thinkers and writers. The problems of the environment reinforce the feeling that all mankind ultimately shares the same fate. The approach to these problems varies greatly, however, and ecological initiatives are severely hampered by inescapable budgetary limitations.

North-South problem areas increase the sense of frustration of the thinking person in the West. What is the future of a planet that is splitting into two halves—a thriving 'Northern' half and a totally impoverished 'Southern' half?

The entire subject of development transcends 19th century ideologies. The countries of South East Asia have indeed succeeded, by importing a Western-style liberal economy, in achieving a spectacular increase in the level of welfare for their populations. But on other continents, neither neocapitalist nor Marxist solutions seem to have produced any results. The widening of the development gap between the prosperous North and the impoverished South constitutes a threat to the Western democracies, not only because of the ethical crisis to which it can give rise, but also in terms of economic and political relations.

This list of the challenges facing our Western society is certainly not exhaustive. There are also the problems posed by our eternal quest for scientific progress, especially in the field of biogenetics and in the case of many other technological discoveries of potentially far-reaching impact on our lives.

The irreversibility of *Perestroika*

Mikhail Gorbachev will surely go down in history as the political leader responsible for the epochal reform movement in the Eastern Bloc countries. The answer to the question: What will be the future evolution of the policy of reform and the process of democratisation? turns on two major factors: first, the political future of Gorbachev himself and the extent to which he can remain the master of events, and secondly, the measure of irreversibility of the liberalisation movement already underway in most communist countries.

What are the clearest criteria of irreversibility? The issue raised by this question is a critical one. Events in China have shown that many reforms can be crushed by military might and that democratisation can be reversed.

The irreversibility of democratic reform can be evaluated on the basis of the following four criteria:

- Establishment of a pluralistic parliamentary democracy based on a multiparty system.
- Strict separation of powers between the legislative, the executive and the judiciary.
- Dismantling of the police apparatus.
- Reduction in the strength of the armed forces.

These four conditions are gradually being met in a number of communist countries and even in the Soviet Union. But they are subject to a precondition—the abandonment of the Brezhnev doctrine—and this, of course, depends on the goodwill of the Soviet leaders.

Probably the entire progressive movement initiated by Gorbachev will stand or fall with the Gorbachev policy. The future of the Kremlin leaders' policy can be analysed on the basis of five scenarios.

- Gorbachev succeeds with the support of the West. The economic situation gradually improves, there is massive disarmament, and the communist countries pursue democratic reforms and engage in co-operation with the Western democracies. The Soviet Union is de-Sovietised and its largest republic becomes Russian once more. The other Soviet republics assume varying degrees of independence.

- Gorbachev fails. One fine day he is removed from his office and *Glasnost* transparency is replaced by frosty opacity. The shock plunges the West into a climate of profound disillusion: disarmament negotiations break down, and there is the threat of resumption of the arms race.

- Gorbachev to maintain his own position, steps up measures restricting the hard-won freedoms. *Glasnost* and *perestroika* are gradually dismantled, and the Gorbachev policy undergoes a drift toward neo-totalitarianism.

The second and third scenarios both threaten to put the lid on the process of democratisation in the countries of Central and Eastern Europe. Even if it seems improbable that, in the event of these scenarios, the Soviet Union would restore communist order by force of arms, it is evident that the leaders in the East would behave far more cautiously, since the fall of Gorbachev would probably reduce them to Soviet-'protectorate' status.

- Gorbachev neither succeeds nor fails. The Soviet Union and the 'satellite' countries experience a period of anarchy and disorder. There is no improvement in the economy; some republics win partial independence. The armed forces and the political leadership are divided on what action to take. The Soviet Union disintegrates. For the West, this would be a particularly precarious situation, since the policy of the Kremlin would be totally unpredictable. Moreover, anarchy increases both the lure and the likelihood of a Bonapartist coup.

- The liberal proponents of a multi-party democracy in the Soviet Union gain increasing numbers of supporters when it appears that the Gorbachev reforms are progressing too slowly and are not going far enough. The Communist Party is converted into a social democratic party, and the Soviet Union follows the Hungarian and Czech models. Under a sub-scenario, a tidal wave of anti-communism engulfs the Soviet Union, propelled in part by the ingrained nationalism of the republics. Opposition to and elimination of the KGB and of communist institutions and leaders might then be more violent. This scenario would tend to resemble what occurred in Romania.

It is clear that for both the people of the Eastern Bloc countries and for the Western world, the first scenario is the only one that holds out adequate hope and is sufficiently constructive.

Western policy should, therefore, be aimed at giving the maximum chances to that scenario.

A new policy of openness toward the East

Events in the Soviet Union and in the Eastern Bloc countries are forcing the countries of the Western world, and more specifically the West European countries, to work out a new policy of openness toward the East. Provided the conditions and circumstances of irreversibility are maintained, this policy should be aimed at converting the de-facto détente between East and West into a structured détente. This presupposes the ending of the Cold War, the emergence of co-operative links between, for instance, NATO and the Warsaw Pact, and the redrawing of links for political co-operation within a Greater Europe. From a Western viewpoint, the political restructuring of Europe should rest on certain planks to promote stability and co-operation:

- The European Economic Community and the continued integration of Europe;

Minister Shevarnadze (USSR) at the Egmont Palace during his visit to Belgium, November 1989.

- NATO, arms control, and a new relationship to include the Warsaw Pact (23 countries);
- The Helsinki process as a guideline for European co-operation (35 countries).

Most important of all, the countries of Western Europe should not be placed in a dilemma that would oblige them to choose between their policy toward the East and their policy toward the West. This dilemma is presented in its most poignant form in the case of the Federal Republic of Germany, which might be obliged to choose between its feeling of solidarity and common destiny for the two Germanies, and its commitment to European integration and the Western defensive alliance. A dilemma of this nature could have fatal consequences for Western European integration and can be avoided only if it is credibly demonstrated that the new policy toward the East is tied to our policy toward Western Europe remaining firmly anchored to its historic goal—the economic and political integration of the European Community.

'Westpolitik'—the basis of a rational 'Ostpolitik' for the 1990's

The new Western policy toward the East can be conducted credibly only if the European Community is strengthened, if the process of integration is completed, and if the Community increasingly appears on the foreign policy stage as a major political power. Relations with the countries of the Eastern Bloc would rapidly deteriorate if the European Community, in its relations with the countries of this Eastern Bloc, were to disintegrate into so many bilateral nationalistic egocentric splinter groups.

The economic collapse of the Eastern Bloc is one of the main causes of the implosion of communism. The credibility of the political reforms will to a great extent be determined by the economic recovery and by the existence of an effective policy to achieve such recovery. Here the European Economic Community has a major role to play. It is no coincidence that the 24 OECD countries have entrusted the European Commission with the co-ordination of aid to the countries of the Eastern Bloc. At the meeting on 19 December 1989, held in Brussels, it was decided to extend this task of co-ordination to cover, in addition to Poland and Hungary, the other East European countries and even the Soviet Union.

Emergency material and financial aid is, of course, of great importance, as are all types of low-interest loans and credits. Nevertheless, it is clear that Western structural support cannot take the place of economic and political reforms in the East Bloc countries which are absolutely essential—democratic political reform and the introduction of a market economy. It is also highly desirable that private finance should start to flow from the West to the countries of the Eastern Bloc. To make this possible, it will be necessary in the short term to develop a guarantee system for private investments, for instance by arranging for the European Bank for Development and Reconstruction (French proposal) to have an export credit guarantee section added to it (Belgian proposal). In the longer term, however, private financing can flourish only if the necessary economic efficiency is provided in the Eastern Bloc countries by the introduction of market economy reforms.

The danger at the moment in all the countries of the Eastern Bloc is that the planned economies will be only partially dismantled, and the market economy only partially introduced, resulting in a sort of witches' brew of contradictions which combines the disadvantages of both systems. It is for this reason that Western aid and co-operation must be made dependent on clear economic and political conditions.

The European Community acts as a role model and thereby exercises a powerful attraction. A slowdown in European integration would badly tarnish that image and lead to profound disillusionment on the part of all those outside the European Community who nurture high expectations for it.

It would be unfortunate for us to fall into a sort of Western Eurocentrism, by which the European Community began to regard itself as the navel of the world. There are, however, such things as a European ideal and European idealism. The frontiers and the geography of Europe are much less important than the geography of the values. These values have to do with democracy, fundamental freedoms, respect for human rights, economic welfare and social justice. Gorbachev said recently that these values have become universal; let us hope that he is right. It cannot be denied, however, that, in their historical development, these values bear an indelible European stamp. Nevertheless, this should not prevent us from admitting that in Europe, not all that long ago, these values and human rights were trodden underfoot in a barbaric manner and on a massive scale.

The ethical and civilised values of Europe are, of course, better served by a democratic and unified Europe than by a mosaic of nations in dispersed order of battle, maintaining allegiance to the 19th century concept of the Nation State.

The great adventure of European integration and unification is undeniably based—perhaps more subconsciously than consciously—on these values of European civilisation which have since acquired universal recognition. The unification of Europe undertaken by the European Community reaches far beyond mere economic, technological, scientific and monetary aspects. This unification is only conceivable, and has therefore only become possible, as a result of the growing European awareness of the existence of what we can call the European spirit.

Alongside the European Community, as the repository of European values of recognised universality, there is also the Council of Europe with its headquarters in Strasbourg which, against the background of the present events and the process of democratisation in Eastern Europe, can play a major role. As soon as fundamental freedoms and rights are re-established in the countries in question, they can become full members of the Council of Europe, and this should contribute substantially to the unification—across national boundaries—of the European continent.

The collapse of communist dictatorship has caused certain nationalistic and integrationist forces to flare up, both in Russia and in the Balkans, with a potentially highly destabilising effect. Here too, Western Europe stands as a model. Franco-German reconciliation and European integration have shown that a common commitment can conquer age-old enmities and atavistic nationalism.

It is important to recognise that democracy and the market economy are two sides of the same coin and that a system of political pluralism,

The European Commission and Council buildings in Brussels.

based on competition between political parties, can flourish only in an environment of economic competition and decentralisation of economic decision-making down to the level of the individual enterprise and the individual consumer. The market economy we are speaking of, however, is not just any market economy but one based on effective competition.

The market economy needs continuous protection against a tendency to self-destruction through the formation of monopolies and cartels. It is precisely for this reason that governments must provide democratic arbitration machinery. The dual concept—democracy and market economy—as described above, inevitably leads to internationalism: technological progress means that economic competition cannot be limited to one country. Great care must be exercised in effecting sociological adjustments and in the development of a consumer-oriented market economy by organising the redistribution of incomes striving for a balance between social expediency and economic efficiency on the basis of political and democratic criteria. The facts prove that in spite of intolerable social injustices which still remain, social progress is best served by democratic market economy societies, particularly if we make the comparison with the individual's lot in communist countries.

If the Western countries attach conditions calling for political and economic reforms to the support given to the Eastern Bloc countries, this is not done with the intention of meddling in the internal affairs of certain countries but is based on the conviction that economic reforms and social progress can succeed only through political and democratic reforms, and the recognition that a democratic society can flourish only in an environment devoid of monopolies, be they political or economic.

The question is frequently put whether the Western world, in setting the conditions linked to its support, is not being more indulgent with the Soviet Union than with the other East European countries, since it recognises that Gorbachev continues to strive for the retention of a one-party system, even though he is attempting within the Communist Party, to move towards a certain degree of democratisation.

The Western World must stand firm on the principle that even in the Soviet Union, political pluralism is, in the long term, the sole guarantee of full respect for human rights and for social and economic progress. But from the Western side, we must also take into account the difficulties in which the Soviet leader finds himself and the fact that the monopoly of the Communist Party in the Soviet Union has for decades constituted the only cement that has held the Soviet Union together. It is understandable that the Kremlin must first find a solution for the nationality problem before consideration can be given to relieving the Communist Party of its monopoly status. But when that moment comes, the West should increase its pressure on this matter.

The European Community is 'a winning concept', and it is not at the moment that we become aware of this that the concept and the reality it embodies should be allowed to atrophy. The work of more than 30 years cannot and must not be destroyed by or even held hostage to the events transpiring in the Eastern Bloc. And the danger of seeing the Community weaken is a very real one.

This danger is mainly an internal one. It is a threat to the Community that has existed from its very inception. A number of Member States still balk at the transfer of any measure of sovereignty. To achieve '1992'—economic and monetary union—will still require a great deal of effort and willingness to compromise among Member States. It is far from certain that all Member States will apply and interpret the Single Act uniformly. And yet, the Single Act clearly sets forth political union as the ultimate goal of the Community. Furthermore, once economic and monetary union has been achieved, political union between the Member States will become almost indispensable if we are to avoid the process of European decision-making becoming the privileged domain of the bureaucracy and of the technocracy and if we intend to establish truly democratic European institutions (the Parliament and the Executive).

It is urgent that the leaders of the Community define the scope of political union[4]. Political union among countries with highly integrated economies, which also comprise a monetary union, is difficult to conceive of without a common foreign policy. In fact, this common foreign policy exists already in part within the framework of European political co-operation (EPC). Such co-operation operates on the basis of unanimity. A common foreign policy, in turn, is difficult to conceive of without a common security doctrine or policy. Currently, the

---

[4] This will be one of the most important tasks of the Conference on Political Union scheduled to open in Rome on 14 December 1990, in parallel with a Conference on Economic and Monetary Union. Both Conferences, convened at the behest of European Community leaders when they met in Dublin in June 1990, are due to conclude by the end of 1992.

security and defence policies of a number of European Member States is co-ordinated within the Western European Union, but this does not seem to be the most effective approach. Of course, the security policy of a European political union can be neither anti-American nor anti-Russian in a climate of unprecedented détente. Instead, it is a European security policy that must give new impetus to NATO: a further aim should be to achieve a co-operative security policy and a security community for a Greater Europe from the Atlantic to the Urals. This is contingent, of course, on the continued pursuit of political reform in the countries of the Eastern Bloc and on continued progress toward détente.

If political union worthy of the name is not forthcoming among the countries of this community—a community whose membership is open—we may find ourselves confronted with two dangerous developments:

- The *de facto* emergence of a shared American-Soviet hegemony over Europe should it appear that the Europeans are not themselves in a position to assume a number of essential responsibilities. Such a Europe is certainly not the Europe the founders of the EEC dreamed of, nor the Europe that can offer coming generations the prospects for their future which should constitute their birthright.

- The effective disintegration of the Warsaw Pact increases the danger of de facto American-Soviet hegemony over Europe. The Soviet Union remains the only party with whom the West can negotiate disarmament since Poland, Hungary, Czechoslovakia and others have already demanded the withdrawal of Soviet troops. This is an internal matter for the countries of the Warsaw Pact. It is increasingly apparent, however, that the current disarmament negotiations which are taking place more and more over the heads of the Europeans could lead to the two superpowers devising a European peace and security system without the countries of Europe having a say in the matter. The only way to avoid this is for the European members of NATO to form a European pillar within the Alliance. The WEU can play a very important role in this regard.

The stagnation of political integration which would lead to decline and would weaken the Community and cause it to lose international credibility. In this situation, Europe would become more a *factor of destabilisation* than of stability and balance. But stability and balance is precisely what the Greater Europe of tomorrow needs. An emasculated European Community, ultimately reduced to the status of an economic free trade zone, would place the European continent under Russian influence to a substantial degree, even if the Soviet Union were to become desovietised and were to acquire economic clout. Only a European Community that has reached maturity will constitute a valid and credible partner for the new Russia, a partner able to establish a relationship in which entente and co-operation can flourish.

The German question

The new policy toward the East and the German question are intimately linked.

The countries of the European Community and the other countries of the Western Alliance, must make it possible for the Federal Republic and its leaders to escape the dilemma of having to choose between the bonds which link them to the people of the GDR and their membership in the European Community and in NATO. On this issue, it should be stated from the outset that the Western partners of the Federal Republic have had no objection in principle to the reunification of Germany. The declaration adopted on this matter during the European Council in Strasbourg on 8 and 9 December 1989 had very broad implications:

> 'We seek the reinforcement of the state of peace in Europe, in which the German people will recover their unity by a process of free self-determination. This process must be achieved pacifically and democratically, in the respect of agreements and treaties, and of all the principles defined by the Final Act of Helsinki, in a context of dialogue and of East–West co-operation. It should also be situated in the perspective of European integration.'

The Malta Summit with Presidents Bush and Gorbachev (USSR).

This declaration contained all the elements needed to allow German reunification to take place on a gradual basis, provided that the process of democratisation in the GDR is pursued, and that the right of self-determination can be exercised democratically. In addition, the countries of the EEC, including the Federal Republic, state that reunification can take place only in full respect of and compliance with existing agreements, conventions and treaties (EEC, NATO and possibly, for the GDR, the Warsaw Pact) and the principles laid down by the Helsinki Final Act.

This last point refers to the sensitive problem of borders: it is agreed that the borders established after World War II must be maintained, and that they can be revised only through negotiation.

Since the events in Eastern Europe, the German leaders have continuously affirmed the FRG's unswerving loyalty to the European Community and to the pursuit of European integration as formulated in the Single Act. It is of capital importance that this courageous and loyal attitude of leading German politicians toward the European Community be endorsed by the Federal Republic elections in December 1990. If the Federal Republic were to give preference to its *Ostpolitik* to the detriment of its bonds with the West, thereby causing the process of integration of Western Europe to lapse into stagnation and decline, this could have tragic consequences for the future of Europe. Not only would 30 years of joint political effort be lost, but there would ensue throughout Europe a senseless 'every-man-for-himself' mentality. A Germany thus reunited but detached from Europe would then become the dominant power in Central Europe and, despite any neutral status, would play a role as arbiter, with a watchful eye on events and attitudes in Eastern Europe and in the Soviet Union. On the world level, Western Europe would then be reduced to a mere fringe area. The United Kingdom would resolidify its privileged relations with the United States and would play Anglo-American solidarity to the hilt in all fields, while France would probably strive for closer ties with the countries of the Mediterranean region. Under this catastrophic scenario, the BENELUX countries would become totally marginalised. Apart from the political consequences, it is clear that a Europe once again fragmented would be in no position to meet the great technological and competitive challenges with which it and the rest of the world will be confronted in the next century.

If the other Europeans expect German leaders to remain steadfast in their loyalty to Europe and in their dedication to the great adventure of European unification, as laid down in the Treaty of Rome and in the Single Act, then the German leaders in turn have a right to expect that the other 11 Member States and their leaders will do nothing to thwart or hinder the reunification of the German people. A way must be found then to reconcile European unification in the spirit of Jean Monnet and German unification as envisaged by Chancellor Kohl.

There are also a number of difficult and delicate questions to which it is not yet possible to offer satisfactory answers. Can reunification of the two Germanys respect the commitments entered into under NATO and under the Warsaw Pact? Does not reunification presuppose negotiations between NATO and the Warsaw Pact, and possible negotiations in the wider context of the Group of 35 (the Helsinki Group)?

Do we not include the risk that, in spite of all good intentions and promises, the Federal Republic will separate from NATO? Can a situation not be envisaged in which, after further substantial progress, détente and disarmament, a co-operative security system would be worked out which would lessen the relevance of the German 'divided loyalties' dilemma? In efforts to achieve greater stability in Europe there have been signs that the Kremlin might ultimately prefer a reunification solution in which current FRG territory would continue to be part of NATO while the territory of the GDR would be demilitarised.

Chancellor Kohl's 10-point plan, although probably intended in the first instance for domestic political consumption, at least has the merit of expressing a coherent vision of a step-by-step approach to the German problem. The idea of a confederation, as proposed by Chancellor Kohl, has some points in common with the concept of a *'Vertragsgemeinschaft'* proposed by the leaders of the GDR. The outcome of free parliamentary elections will be all-important, just as they will be elsewhere in Eastern Europe.

Most of the governments are still wholly, or partly, in communist hands, and it is clear that the communists, whether or not regrouped under the label of a so-called 'new party', are making efforts to retain some of their power and even to maintain the police apparatus, albeit under a new guise.

The situation in the GDR at the internal political level clearly differs from that in countries such as Poland, Hungary and even Czechoslovakia. In the latter countries, even under communist domination—political opposition with its strengths and its weaknesses—was already organised. But in the GDR the communist monopoly was absolute and brooked no opposition. The Liberal Party and the CDU, which existed on paper in the GDR, were merely the puppets of the régime, which in fact financed them. As a result, the opposition in the GDR experienced great difficulty in organising itself. Particularly alarming is the continuing lack of experience in political and economic matters.

President Gehrlach, Chairman of the Liberal Party, told me that he wanted the GDR to remain a socialist society, retaining state ownership and the means of production and maintaining state planning for large firms. The market economy would thus only be available to small and medium-size firms (SMCs). Concepts like this lead to economic chaos. European leaders who oppose the direct introduction of capitalism, forget that the economic system of the West has gone through a very radical change in the last 50 years, and that what they call 'capitalism' has in fact evolved into a mixed economy in which government expenditure, through a substantial redistribution of income, in most cases now represents 50-60 per cent of GNP compared to a bare 10 per cent before World War I. In any event, the economic learning curve in the countries of Eastern Europe will be a long one; it will entail a continuous battle against a host of misconceptions.

During 1990, parliamentary elections will have been held in both the Federal Republic and in the GDR. The unification of Germany entered a decisive phase when the GDR acquired a democratically elected government.

The electoral victory of the 'Allianz' and of the CDU and the formation in the GDR of a government with a two-third's majority, able to amend its constitution, means that reunification can be expected to take place in the framework of Article 23 of the FRG constitution. Under that article, the GDR, already divided into 'Länder', will join the Federal Republic and the whole country will simply become 'Germany'. This solution is obviously the best one from the Western viewpoint, since it would result in the current territory of the GDR becoming an integral part of the European Community without having to go through the long and complicated procedure of applying for membership. The directives of the European Community, already applicable to the Federal Republic, will automatically be extended to the whole of a reunited Germany. This solution would also facilitate the continuation of reunified Germany within NATO, provided that the Soviet Union can be persuaded to drop its opposition to this.[5]

---

[5] Following the publication by NATO heads of state and government, on 6 July 1990, of the London Declaration on a Transformed North Atlantic Alliance, and two days of talks between Chancellor Helmut Kohl and the Soviet leadership in Moscow on 15 and 16 July, President Gorbachev announced that the Soviet Union accepted that a united Germany would be a member of the Alliance. NATO welcomed this development, emphasising that Germany's membership in the Alliance would increase stability for all. NATO Secretary General Manfred Wörner also visited Moscow from 13 to 16 July to hold discussions with President Gorbachev.

In March 1990, reacting to positions taken on German reunification and especially to President Gorbachev's statements that a unified Germany could not be a member of NATO, I stressed that the unification of the two Germanies and the unification of the European Community must proceed in parallel. It will be hard to explain how monetary union can be created between the two Germanies (as happened on 1 July 1990), despite the major economic differences that exist between the Federal Republic and the GDR, while the process of establishing Economic and Monetary Union among the 12 Member States of the EC continues to move two steps forwards and one step backwards.

Now is the time to seize a historical opportunity to build a European foundation. In a broader co-operative European context, this could become a credible partner for the countries of Central and Eastern Europe, as well as for the Soviet Union and, of course, for the United States. The roles played by a united Germany, by the United Kingdom and by France within the European Community will be of major importance in this context. However, the smaller countries of Europe can and must also play an important role in the 'ultimate federation' of the European Community. This does not mean that the Community must not be open to other candidates for Community membership, provided the requisite conditions are met.

When it comes to the building of a Community for European Security, NATO, as an existing and dynamic security organisation, constitutes an extremely important factor. That is why it is highly desirable for a united Germany to be a member of NATO. As a multilateral defence organisation, NATO is a factor for stability in the developing relationship with the Soviet Union.

Over the coming months, Soviet officials will have to be persuaded that having a united Germany in NATO also constitutes a substantial advantage from their own standpoint. This will only be possible if the countries of the West offer the Soviet Union a comprehensive package of confidence—and security-building measures.

On 8 March 1990, I published a 14 point programme in which I enumerated those measures which I believe would do most to foster confidence and security between the European countries and the USSR.

1. Speedy conclusion of the CFE negotiations on conventional force reductions in Vienna and the signing in the Autumn of 1990 of an agreement between the 16 Member States of NATO and the 7 Member States of the Warsaw Pact.

   Simultaneously, a second round of negotiations should be started, leading eventually to a further reduction in arms ceilings (CFE II) and a restructuring of the defence system.
2. An acknowledgement that the profound modification of relations between Eastern and Western Europe, insofar as the new situation is irreversible, renders out of date the modernisation of short range missiles (SNF), the directed against targets in Eastern Europe. This new context will require NATO to re-examine this issue.
3. An agreement between the superpowers on a drastic reduction of strategic nuclear arms (START), the elimination of chemical weapons and the conclusion of a treaty on mutual aerial inspection (Open Skies).
4. Concerted action between the members of NATO and of the Warsaw Pact—in consultation with the Western European Union—on verification and implementation of the disarmament process in Europe.
5. The activation of the Helsinki or CSCE process (the Conference on Security and Co-operation in Europe which involves 35 countries including the United States and Canada), including the elaboration of an organised structure for dialogue between these countries at the level of Ministers (with a permanent secretariat). With the support of the United States of America and the USSR, this structure can become very important in establishing a Pan-European security community.
6. A commitment by the Western countries to the effect that after the unification of both Germanies, no NATO troops will be stationed on former East German territory. This can be combined with a gradual withdrawal of Soviet troops.
7. Early announcement by the international community of their intention to confirm the Oder-Neisse line as the border between Germany and Poland.

8. The problem of the German minorities, as well as of all other ethnic minorities in the countries of Central and Eastern Europe and in the Soviet Union, ought to be solved by the strict application of the principles enshrined in the third basket of the Final Act of Helsinki dealing with human rights. This implies that all ethnic minorities should enjoy fundamental rights and freedoms in the field of culture, language, education, religion etc., without modification of borders but with political structures guaranteeing their autonomy in these matters (compare this with the reform of the Belgian State, which bases the autonomy of the different communities on individual cultural and linguistic identity).
9. The conclusion of a peace treaty between the unified Germany and the other countries involved in the Second World War.
10. An offer by NATO of a non-aggression pact with the Soviet Union which would provide, inter alia, structures for co-operation between the countries of Western, Central and Eastern Europe in a number of different fields. This could result in a 'common security charter'.
11. Early implementation of the co-operation agreement between the European Community and the Soviet Union.
12. The establishment of an effective intergovernmental structure for co-operation, in the form of a confederation between the countries of Western, Central and Eastern Europe. Nothing would prevent Member States of this confederation being able to meet the necessary conditions from joining the European Community. An essential element of the concept of confederation is that a federal European Community, as an integrated whole, speaking with one voice, would become a member of the confederation.
13. Through détente, leading to entente, promotion of a Europe of common values (embracing the Soviet Union as well) which would include political democracy based on a multi-party system, a constitution, the separation of powers, basic political, economic and social rights and freedoms, a social market economy, the values of the common European cultural heritage, and values relating to the environment. While

encouraging a market economy in the countries of Central and Eastern Europe, the necessity of a social policy should be underlined (for example by means of a social security system).

14. On a more modest level, Belgium's establishment of an Institute for the Study of Peace and Security can also contribute to the strengthening of mutual confidence. This Institute will enhance inter-university research but will also attract highly qualified experts from East and West. As an international think-tank, the Institute could make a substantial contribution in bringing together the new ideas which are beginning to emerge in a Europe freed from the Cold War.

Security policy

The new policy towards the East presupposes a new approach to defence policy. Conversely, arms control and disarmament entail a new policy toward the East and a new outlook for East–West relations.

The greatest effort must be made to bring the ongoing disarmament talks between East and West to a successful conclusion as soon as possible. The principal fora are the START talks on strategic weapons, the negotiations on a chemical weapons ban, and the CFE negotiations on conventional weapons. It is hoped that agreement can be reached in these three areas in the course of 1990.

The signing of a CFE agreement between the 23 countries of NATO and the Warsaw Pact is expected to serve as the occasion to invite the other countries of the Helsinki Group to exchange ideas among the 35 nations with a view to a subsequent phase of disarmament negotiations.

Present developments in Europe make it improbable that modernisation of short range missiles (LANCE) with nuclear warheads will come up for discussion. For the Federal Republic, this issue seems to be an insuperable one.

The CFE agreement on conventional disarmament is of capital importance for the West since it is the first time an attempt is being made to end the substantial imbalance that exists in favour of the Warsaw Pact and the Soviet Union. From what is now on the table in

Vienna, it appears that about 94,000 weapons with an offensive capability are to be eliminated and that troop strength is to be reduced.

The extensive verification and control measures that are to accompany this could form a basis for co-operation between NATO and the Warsaw Pact. On the Western side, the CFE accord will not lead initially to substantial budgetary savings.

If the Gorbachev policy can be pursued in the countries of the Eastern Bloc, there will be room for even more far-reaching disarmament and arms reduction talks. It should be borne in mind that, even after the CFE agreement, which it is hoped will be concluded in 1990, NATO and the Warsaw Pact will together still have in excess of 40,000 tanks, 30,000 pieces of artillery, 50,000 armoured vehicles and 10 million troops.

From the standpoint of a peace policy which seeks to establish a period of peace and security in Europe, neither armament nor disarmament is an end in itself. The key issue is at what level can a cost-effective defence be achieved that will guarantee the maintenance of peace and stability.

With this in mind, the concept of a 'mutual defensive defence posture' can be advanced.

A defensive defence posture of capability means reducing the military arsenal to a level that makes massive aggression no longer possible. Military capability is therefore the key. This does not mean that the intentions behind a security policy are unimportant, especially in a democracy where the government has to answer to Parliament. From its inception, NATO has been a defensive alliance of democratic nations, established during the period which Paul Henri Spaak called 'la grande peur', when the Stalin régime in the Soviet Union began to annex one country after another in Eastern Europe and to subject them to the dictatorship of the Kremlin. Despite the arms race, NATO has always emphasized its exclusively defensive role and has always made clear that NATO forces would never be the first to initiate hostilities.

A defensive defence posture can under no circumstances be adopted unilaterally since to do so would create asymmetry and imbalance, thereby destroying stability, one of the essential conditions.

It should be stressed, moreover, that a defensive defence capability and a nuclear deterrent are not incompatible. An adequate defensive defence posture must be sufficiently deterring and must be capable of neutralising any attack from outside. In a world in which nuclear weapons continue to proliferate, an exlusively defensive posture without a nuclear deterrent component would not be adequate for Europe. If this reasoning is valid for NATO forces in Europe, it is obviously equally valid for the Warsaw Pact countries.

It is sophistry to assert that a nuclear-free Europe would necessarily be safer than a Europe in which modern weapons—including nuclear — would provide a minimum defence.

Maintaining a nuclear component as part of strategic doctrine by no means implies that the component must involve short-range missiles. Great Britain and France each has its own nuclear strike force. Further progress in European integration would make it desirable for these countries to bring their nuclear capability, in one way or another, into the European Union. Defence solidarity with the United States within NATO must also be maintained.

A steady improvement in East–West relations in the field of disarmament must evolve through a substantial reduction by both sides in weapons and troop levels, into a 'mutually reinforcing exclusively defensive posture'.

At the same time, we must seek to develop an East–West cooperative security policy covering such aspects as arms control and verification and the development of an early warning system against surprise attack, as well as other confidence building measures.

In this perspective, it should be possible to reassess the Harmel doctrine and give it a meaning that corresponds to the new situation. We might speak of the need to formulate a new Harmel doctrine.

In the view of the Harmel report, the political and strategic attitudes of NATO should be based upon military deterrence, on the one hand, and on negotiations which, if they succeeded, must lead to détente, on the other. The Harmel doctrine, applied successfully by NATO over the years, proves abundantly that NATO has always been a politico-military alliance in which the political component has been foremost.

In the current context, the political component must be reinforced still further.

A neo-Harmel or even post-Harmel approach, on the assumption of an end to the Cold War, might be formulated as follows:

THE IMPLOSION OF COMMUNISM

The Soviet Foreign Minister, Mr Shevarnadze, with Mr Wörner during their talks at the NATO headquarters at Evere (Brussels) on December 19th, 1989.

disarmament plus assistance to the reform movement in Eastern Europe equals détente and heightened co-operation, accompanied by a whole series of confidence building measures leading ultimately to solid entente. The establishment by the countries of NATO and the Warsaw Pact of a consultative body to deal with security matters of common interest could constitute a major confidence building measure.

The Helsinki Final Act (35 countries) which crowned the Conference for Security and Co-operation in Europe; the final documents of the review conferences in Belgrade, Madrid and Vienna; and the Stockholm agreement—all of these collectively have initiated a process which could culminate in the formation of a European Security and Co-operation Community.

The other countries of the 35-strong Helsinki Group will probably be invited to the signing in Vienna this year of the CFE disarmament agreement among the 23 NATO and Warsaw Pact countries.

It is desirable that advantage be taken of this occasion to provide a new impetus to broader disarmament negotiations, within the security and co-operation machinery under Basket I of the Helsinki Final Act.

According to many observers, Basket II, which deals with economic and scientific co-operation, is not being fully utilised. The conference to be held on this subject this year in Bonn, and the prospects offered by the United Nations Economic Commission for Europe should, between them, be able to fill this gap.*

In 1992 there will be a new Helsinki review conference. If détente between East and West continues, this conference can take on decisive significance in restructuring the political geography of Europe. This geography will be determined to a great extent by:

- the relations between NATO and the Warsaw Pact and the state of progress in disarmament and arms control talks;
- the process of democratisation in the countries of the Eastern Bloc and the development of relations between the Federal Republic and the GDR;
- the possible adoption of a number of concrete confidence building measures, especially as regards the post-World War II Oder-Neisse line, the unalterability and inviolability of which must be unequivocally reaffirmed;
- to crown the détente process, the conclusion of a peace agreement with the two Germanies or with the political entity these countries may have then become;
- the conclusion between NATO and the Warsaw Pact of mutual and effective non-aggression treaties;
- the development of various integration projects among groups of European countries.

---

* The Bonn Conference on Economic Co-operation in Europe took place from 19 March to 11 April 1990 and enabled a significant progress to be made. The principle objectives set by western participants were achieved, including progress and the question of private property ownership and its impact on economic co-operation.

The Soviet Union and the United States both have a major responsibility in restructuring the political map of Europe, if only as co-signatories of the Helsinki Final Act. Secretary of State Baker, during a speech given in Berlin on 12 December 1989, set out the broad outlines of the American view on tomorrow's Europe. It is worthy of note that, after stressing the solidarity of NATO and the importance of the Helsinki process, the Secretary of State strongly emphasised the importance of maintaining and pursuing European integration. It also appears that the United States has been won over to the idea of anchoring German reunification to the European Community and to the process of European unification, and wants the special relationship between the EEC and the United States to be given institutional form.

The new political map of Europe

The greatest confidence and hope for the future centres on the European Community. Before 1992, the eve of the Single Market, opinions should converge on the concrete content of the economic and monetary union and on the scope of the future political union. Only a stronger Europe will enable the EEC to respond to the requests for aid and co-operation assistance from the countries of the Eastern Bloc and from the countries of the Southern Hemisphere.

It is imperative that co-operation with the six EFTA countries be strengthened and be given a new form. These negotiations will start in 1990 in the hope of reaching early agreement on solutions to common problems for separate implementation by the EEC and by the EFTA countries. Machinery for monitoring joint EEC-EFTA decisions could take the form of admitting EFTA judges to sit on the European Court of Justice and setting up a joint Parliamentary Assembly consisting of a delegation from the European Parliament and delegations from the EFTA Parliaments.

The economic identity of interests between the EEC and EFTA has become very substantial.

Exports from the EEC countries to EFTA are more than the combined exports from the EEC countries to the United States and Japan. A structure must be developed for co-operation with the EFTA countries that extends beyond mere association. We might speak of a

On 12 and 13 February 1990 the Ministers of Foreign Affairs of NATO and Warsaw Pact countries convened at the Ottawa Conference.

European Economic Zone (EEZ). This concept would acquire even more content if it were structured on a confederation basis which, although embracing 18 countries, would envisage membership status for the European Community as an international entity, and possibly for EFTA.

Under the Treaty of Rome, the European Community is an open community; this means that countries of the EFTA group can also become full members, provided that they accept the Community as it now stands and accept political unity as the Community's ultimate goal. This, in turn, entails a partial transfer of sovereignty, the pursuit of a common foreign policy, and the acceptance of decisions by the required majority. Nor can the possibility be excluded *a priori* that countries which today belong to the Group of Twelve and which have difficulty in accepting greater political integration in the European Community might, at some point, elect to transfer to the looser confederation.

As regards the countries of the Eastern Bloc, it is clear that they must first advance further down the path of democratisation and economic recovery before specific co-operative links, such as association, can be considered. It is clear, however, that if efforts at democratisation and economic reform are successful, certain countries of Central and Eastern Europe could also be considered for a closer form of association in a future European confederation.[6]

Inasmuch as we are approaching the convening of a conference of the 35 nations of the Helsinki Group on the occasion of the signing of a CFE agreement, it is most important that the EC Twelve go to that conference armed with as clear a vision as possible of the political future of the European Community.

The relationships between the European Community, once it forms a political union, and the member countries of what will constitute a Pan-European confederation, poses a series of delicate problems. What if the Soviet Union or certain of the Republics that currently are part of the Soviet Union, were to ask to join the Pan-European federation? What, in the ultimate analysis, is our definition of Europe—culturally, politically, and economically? And if substantial portions of the Soviet Union were to form an integral part of a European structure—Europe from the Atlantic to the Urals—what attitude should we then adopt toward the United States, which remains steadfast in its intent to establish an institutional link with the European Community?

---

[6] Possibly with the EEC itself, if all the conditions were met.

Here we must give the German Federal Republic enough latitude to develop a '*sui generis*' form of co-operation with the GDR capable of evolving into *de facto* unification. Nor should we forget that since the foundation of the European Community 30 years ago, the GDR has always, through the Federal Republic, maintained a very special economic relationship with the European Community.

On 16 November 1989, I spoke for the first time in '*De Standaard*' of the possibility of structuring the European economic space as a confederation—as it happens before either Chancellor Kohl, in his 10-point programme, or President Mitterrand, in his New Year's message, had advanced the idea.

The concept of a great confederation, based on the pillars of the EEC, EFTA and COMECON, doubtless involves the danger that the specific nature of the European Community might be lost in such an association. In any case, the EEC is the only truly integrated group of countries with supra-national authority transferred to Community institutions. It must therefore be made clear at the outset that the European Community can belong to this confederation as an entity, but that individual Member States may not, because to allow that would expose the Community to a diminution in its authority. A European confederation open to countries which are dedicated members of the European Community makes sense only if the Community itself evolves into a confederation and can, as a confederation, play a dynamic role within this larger confederation, without having to abandon its own specific identity.

North-South relations

The evolution of East–West relations and the lengths to which the countries of the West have gone to encourage the reforms in the countries of Eastern Europe and to give them economic, financial and technical assistance, fill the leaders of Third World countries with the concern that all this aid may be given at the expense of development aid for the countries of the Third World. Those leaders are frequently heard to complain that the whites are busy helping other whites in the North, and that the South is the victim of this process. This attitude immediately places at issue the credibility of Western policy towards the developing countries. A clear answer must be given to this challenge.

The European Community must be judged on the basis of its deeds. A new Lome Agreement has just been concluded; Lome IV increases the financial support package from 7.5 billion to 12 billion ECU in addition a number of credit arrangements.*

Lome IV represents a significant improvement in the quality of aid by introducing greater flexibility to adapt to the local situation.

It is far better for the countries of the Third World to have to deal with a strong European Community than with a European Community lacking in unity and threatened with fragmentation and weakness. For Third World countries too, a stronger Europe is better than a weaker Europe. It would be advisable, for example, for the Lome Agreements, in time, to be financed, from a European tax, such as an excise duty on petrol in Europe, as a meaningful symbol of solidarity. A decision of this kind could only be taken, however, by the European Parliament which, as of now, lacks the requisite authority.

It should also be noted that economic recovery in the countries of Eastern Europe could open new export markets to the countries of the Third World. The countries of Eastern Europe may also be able to assume their responsibilities in the field of development co-operation.

East–West détente should lead to significant arms reductions which in future, with CFE II, could go even beyond what is foreseen today. This, in the longer term, will undoubtedly make it possible to fund development aid with budgetary resources freed by savings on military expenditure. This would open the way to the possibility of negotiating a 'Pact for Joint Growth' with those developing countries interested in such an agreement. I made just such a proposal at the 1979 (UNCTAI) Conference, but the economic crisis at the end of the Seventies and the first half of next decade completely overshadowed the North-South dialogue and made any discussion on more automatic machinery for the transfer of financial resources to developing countries impossible.

---

* The Lome Convention of 31 October 1979 established the contractual relationship between the EEC and the African, Caribbean and Pacific (ACP) states to promote trade and economic co-operation between the ACP states and the Community and between the ACP states themselves. The convention has been renewed on three occasions, most recently on 17 December 1989.

East–West détente can also open the way for more expeditions and more effective solutions to regional conflicts on the other continents; such conflicts consume substantial resources and often take a high toll in human lives. Peaceful settlement by negotiation of such conflicts, without intervention by the superpowers, also opens up favourable prospects for development co-operation.

Finally, it should be mentioned that the developing countries have an obligation to themselves to make a start on arms control and on the reduction of military expenditures, at a time when East and West are about to reduce substantially their overall armaments effort.

Expenditure on arms by the countries of the Third World amounts to about 160 billion dollars a year, which is four times greater than the total amount of official development aid granted by the North to the South. These figures point to the urgent necessity of pursuing disarmament with the same determination on all continents.

'1990'

After the euphoria of 1989—the collapse of the communist dictatorships one after the other and the universal popular rejoicing—1990 threatened to be the year of anticlimax and of return to hard reality.

It will very soon appear—and is in fact already appearing—that economic recovery in the countries of Eastern Europe is very complex, is not going fast enough, and that the regained political freedom is not a miracle cure that fills the shops with goods and raises the standard of living. Political reforms toward greater democracy are a necessary condition for economic recovery, but not unfortunately, a sufficient condition. After the high expectations, public opinion in the countries of Central and Eastern Europe will have to endure great disappointments and accept harsh realities. The communist parties will take advantage of this to say that things weren't all that bad under communist dictatorship. This sort of talk may be implausible, but it is likely to confuse public opinion and thus the voters, in their bewilderment, could lose confidence in more democratic régimes.

In the GDR and Romania—and to a lesser extent in Bulgaria and Czechoslovakia—the communist parties are attempting to improve their image and to retain substantial segments of power. These efforts will intensify as disillusionment among the population deepens.

Even the support of the West to Eastern Europe will not prove capable of improving the situation substantially. Only structural political and economic reforms can alter the orientation of these societies fundamentally. There is a real danger, however, that the lack of a spectacular economic recovery will be ascribed by the East European leaders to the procrastination and shilly-shallying of the West.

The situation in the Soviet Union could take a decisive turn in the course of the coming months. For Gorbachev, it is imperative that he find an institutional solution to the nationality problem by the introduction of an all-embracing loose confederation. If economic *perestroika* fails to produce concrete results, Gorbachev's political position will be increasingly imperilled. The consequences of such a failure would be dramatic. The peoples of Eastern Europe would probably oppose with violence any attempt by the Kremlin to deprive them of the freedoms so valiantly won.

For the European Community, 1990 will have been another decisive year on both the internal and external fronts.

As regards progress toward the Single European Market, movement of capital was liberalised on 1 July 1990; before the end of the year we will see the start of the intergovernmental conference to work out the arrangements for economic and monetary union and to extend the jurisdiction of the European Parliament. Nor can formulation of the basis for political union be long delayed.

The unity of the European Community and its ultimate objective can be placed in jeopardy by the events in Eastern Europe, by the tendency to give preference to Ostpolitik, and the evolution of the German problem. Greater democracy, greater freedom, greater security, greater prosperity and greater welfare, are possible only through a stronger Europe. To achieve this, requires even greater attachment to the European ideal and to European idealism.

The French politician and author Benjamin Constant, renowned for his cynicism, wrote 150 years ago:

'*L'homme échappe au passé parce qu'il l'oublie, et croit posséder l'avenir parce qu'il l'ignore*'.

'Man escapes his past through his forgetfulness and through his ignorance believes that the future is his'.

I think that today we cannot escape the past, a past that has often been of tragic dimensions but that has known moments of human

The European Flag.

greatness as well. The future does not bear a mathematical equivalence to either the past or the present. It is different, even if it grows pell-mell out of what has happened and what has not happened. We do not have the future in our power, it is not a vested right. But we can have an influence upon it, for good or for ill.

The pace of history in recent months is indeed breathtaking. But hopefully, out of the rubble of the demolished wall, will arise the spirit of rebirth that will enable us to chart our course to greater well-being for current and for future generations.

2. The Necessity of European Union

It has been stated repeatedly that the Europe of the Twelve is one of the key factors in the upheavals which our continent is currently undergoing. The future of the European Community is therefore obviously the right place to start this chapter. I am convinced that it is that future which is about to be decided in the period we have now entered.

The Community has a very full agenda. In broad outline this is as follows:

The Internal Market

The internal market has to be completed in accordance with the legislative programme promulgated in the Commission's 1985 White Paper. As the Single Act requires, the Commission submits regular reports on implementation. However, if we intend to fulfil what we have set out to achieve within the time we have given ourselves, the major portion of the task has to be carried out in 1990 and 1991. In 1992 we will be fully occupied with translating the programme into national legislation. Any attempt to reopen the more difficult issues at this stage would therefore be dangerous—the snowball effect at the end of the exercise would simply be too great. We have about two years—in parliamentary terms that means four to five European Councils. In other words, without taking any credit away from the Internal Market Council and other so-called technical councils which have been doing a remarkable job, we must now consider imposing political constraints and adopting deadlines in order to avoid serious problems when the end of 1992 comes. That means that we must prepare now for the negotiation of Economic and Monetary Union at the end of 1991. The Delors Report is the centre-piece of the Inter-governmental Conference convened by the European Council in Strasbourg to address this issue. Nevertheless every one knows that the negotiations will be difficult and that the stakes are extremely high.

Another field where, like the Single Market, close monitoring is required, is the Community's activity on the labour front. This was highlighted by the Charter adopted by eleven countries in Strasbourg in December 1989, to be implemented by the Commission over the coming months through an action programme. It marks the opening of a new chapter of Community activity.

Faced with such a heavy programme, it might be tempting to say enough is enough. We should not overload the boat. That is not a view I share. We are living through one of those key moments in history—a matter of a few months or a few years—in the course of which the future of several decades is being written.

The nearest parallel is probably the immediate post-war period, 1945-1947, which saw the birth, separated only by a few months, of NATO, of the Coal and Steel Community (forerunner of the EEC) and of the Council of Europe, and the beginnings of the WEU. The multilateral structures which have provided the basis of our foreign policy for the past 45 years were born shortly after the start of the immediate post war period and under the menace of Stalinism. We now have to deal with what Spaak called his 'unfinished battles'[1]. If he had been told that he was taking on too much or 'overloading the boat' by dealing simultaneously with security, coal and steel, economics, democracy and cultural values, he would have probably just shrugged his shoulders. We should do the same. It is not a question of making a conscious decision to deal with so much at the same time. The rapid pace of events demands various responses

---

[1] Paul-Henri Spaak (1899-1972) European statesman, Belgian Minister of Foreign Affairs and Prime Minister in successive governments from the 1930s to the 1960s. Secretary General of NATO from 1957-1961.

simultaneously. Just as in the post-war period, we can expect the decisions we now take and the course we now set to have a lasting effect for generations. Of course we must think long and hard before we act but we must not abstain from taking action just because there are already too many problems to deal with.

What are these events which today are closing in on us? Some are the result of developments within the Community; others come from without. Outside the Community the major concern is the metamorphosis of the European political situation—unthinkable a few short months ago—which threatens to water down the process of European integration within the European Community. In a short space of time, Eastern Europe has seen the collapse of seemingly cast-iron structures, the disavowal of the most monolithic concepts and the crumbling of the most impenetrable of walls. The whole of Europe has been plunged into uncertainty. The result has been so much conjecture over future structures that a new concept has entered our political vocabulary—the future 'European architecture'. The European Community emerges from all this as a pillar of stability which offers East and West a model for reconciliation between nations and peoples and provides a blueprint for economic prosperity. It must be hard, from an Eastern European perspective, to appreciate the day to day reality of the Community, to realise its limitations and to understand the scale of the effort needed to get as far as we have. From a distance, it must seem that we are more united, wealthier and more active than we really are. So much the better, since it is vital that the Community is perceived not only in Brussels but also in Budapest, Moscow, Washington and Tokyo as a major actor on the political stage of tomorrow's Europe. Nevertheless, the Community still has to accelerate and strengthen the process of integration, and reaffirm and give concrete form to the political objectives enshrined in the treaties from the outset. This also means equipping itself with effective machinery for dealing with external matters.

The alternative is not an encouraging one—a return to the Europe of nations of the pre-war years, inevitable loss of political and economic influence, and precious little to guarantee stability in the field of external security.

In addition to this outside challenge—one which would have interested Toynbee[2].—The pace of the Community's internal development has obviously increased.

The rapid establishment of the principal elements of the Internal Market, the unhoped for advances in the dialogue on Economic and Monetary Union, and the feeling which has characterised the life of the community for the past few years that the market has acquired a new dynamism—all these have given rise to new concerns and new objectives. Concerns tend to fall into three categories—fear of a technocratic bureaucracy; fear of economic determinism; and fear of the shift of power to the centre. What is in fact meant, when people refer to shortcomings in the democratic process, is that powers acquired, often at heavy cost, over the centuries by our democratically elected national parliaments might be bereft of substance if key decisions are to be taken in future at the European level, under procedures which would give too much power to national and Community bureaucracies. There are legitimate concerns about the creation of a 'technocratic' Europe. There are worries too about the primarily economic and technical character of the European treaties, which for understandable historical reasons have been unable to deal *in extenso* with the various aspects of social welfare legislation. The success of the process of European construction—seemingly dormant for so long—has itself led member countries to query the limits of the undertaking and the implications for the maintenance of their own authority. In other words there is a feeling that we are approaching the limits of the transfer of sovereignty. This explains the fear of a centralised bureaucracy and the growing support for the principle of 'subsidiarity' (see below).

These, it seems to me, are the challenges confronting the Community, both from within and from without—challenges which must be swiftly met, not just because we are in a hurry but because we are being driven by events. If it is to stay credible, the Community must improve

---

[2] Arnold Toynbee, Director of Studies of the Royal Institute of International Affairs, London 1925-1955. In 'A Study of History' (12 volumes) published between 1934 and 1961, he attempted to discover the laws governing the rise and fall of civilisations.

its internal decision-making process and at the same time mobilise and expand its capability for dealing with external matters. To retain the support of the nations and of the peoples of which it is actually made up—and therein resides its ultimate legitimacy—the Community must strengthen the democratic character of its internal processes for reaching decisions and be seen to respect the rights of the individual as well as those of the Member States.

That is the background against which one has to look at the issues facing the institutions of the Community. These come under four headings: effectiveness, democracy, 'subsidiarity', and political unity.

Effectiveness

This is a matter which relates primarily to the European Council of Ministers, the Commission and the European Parliament. It was the combined extension of the powers of these three institutions which lay behind the success of the Single Act and the Internal Market. The instruments for bringing this about were the introduction, on a much broader basis than hitherto, of the principle of the 'qualified majority' in the Council; the institution of procedures for co-operation with the Parliament; and giving the Commission the power to execute its decisions in practice as well as in theory.

We have to continue to work along these lines.

The Council has now had several years of operating under the Single Act. The experience has shown that in fields where the 'qualified majority' applies, decision-making is effective and timely. That is true of several sectors of the internal market. Bottlenecks arise in fields where unanimity is still required. Fiscal matters are one such area, but there are others. The obvious conclusion is to make the qualified majority the general rule for all decisions within the broad scope of the European treaties, particularly in areas such as environmental protection and social welfare, where the rule does not presently apply. If we have to conclude that some exceptions are inevitable, we must keep these to a strict minimum. In principle unanimity should only be required in future for constitutional matters such as amendments to the Treaty of Rome, decisions about applications for membership, and measures taken in accordance with Article 235[3]. This would represent a further step in the progressive development of the Community of which the Single Act was one part.

The executive power of the Commission, based on Article 155[4] of the Treaty, has long been a stumbling block. The Single Act has helped us to achieve some progress but there are endless examples of the gap between practice and theory. There has to be a serious effort to limit the use of delegation procedures as well as the number of cases where the Council specifically reserves powers to itself—and in fact violates the spirit of the Treaty in so doing.

The other important element is the reinforcement of the authority of the President of the Commission. Without impairing the collegiate nature of that institution, it seems essential, from an operational point of view, that the President of the Commission should become, increasingly, *'primus inter pares'*. One way of achieving this might be for the President to be elected by the European Parliament on the basis of an absolute majority. Candidates would be proposed by the Council of Ministers. This would give the President dual legitimacy, having been nominated by the Council, which acts as the guarantor of the interests of Member States and ensures balance; and having had his nomination approved by a majority in the democratically elected assembly. It would have to be agreed that the President thus elected would exercise a key influence on the fair distribution of portfolios within the Commission. That would ensure that, through his contacts with Member States, he would have a genuine influence on the selection of candidates. The result would be a smaller, more cohesive and therefore more effective team, but the range of nationalities and opinions represented within it would be safeguarded. In any case it is generally conceded that at some stage the number of commissioners will have to be reduced.

---

[3] Article 235 of the Treaty of Rome makes provision for action by the Council in circumstances in which the Treaty has not provided the necessary powers for an objective of the Community to be attained.

[4] Article 155 states inter alia that the Commission shall 'have its own power of decision and participate in the shaping of measures taken by the Council and by the European Parliament . . .'

With regard to the Court of Justice, this is a Community institution whose influence on Europe's future tends to be underestimated, despite the frequent contributions it has made. During the past few years, its authority has occasionally been questioned because Member States have failed to take appropriate action to implement its rulings.

Fortunately these are isolated cases but I regret to say that it has involved Belgium too. Legal minds should apply themselves to finding ways of ensuring better compliance. Relevant provisions could be written into the Treaty if need be.

Democracy

You cannot talk about democracy without considering the role of Parliament. This is where, in the European context, we have to act with the greatest resolve if we are serious about strengthening the democratic character of the Community. And this cannot be achieved without increasing the legislative powers of the European Parliament.

How does it operate and exercise its powers at present? For quite some time now, there has been a mechanism for consulting the Parliament on areas where unanimity between Member States is required. This procedure was extended under the Single Act. There is also a procedure for dialogue, for which there is no provision in the Treaty but which stems from declarations of intent made by the Council or the Commission or by the European Parliament itself.

In both cases, it has to be said, the Parliament's influence on decisions has been limited. The Single Act was something of a new departure and introduced a co-operative arrangement between the European Parliament and the Council which enables the Parliament to be associated with the decision-making process. For example, it can modify a position taken by the Council, but the latter retains the ultimate power of decision. This applies particularly to the Internal Market but works in other fields as well. I see no reason why this procedure should not be extended to include all Community legislation. It would remove a number of anomalies. The co-operative procedure does not currently apply to the free circulation of services, nor to the field of transport, for example, although no valid reason has been given for this.

Secondly the role of the Parliament might be extended to include giving its assent to important decisions such as amendments to the Treaty, proposals by the Commission to establish its own resources, approval of major international treaties, and the introduction of uniform electoral procedures for the Parliament itself. Under constitutional law in the majority of our countries, these are all matters which call for parliamentary approval. Why should not the same apply to the European Parliament? As things are, the need for its assent is limited to a few exceptions such as the admission of new members, or association agreements.

One of the most telling criticisms which can be levelled against current legislative procedures under the Single Act is that they permit the Council to approve a measure at the second reading even if an absolute majority in the Parliament opposes it. However hypothetical a case this might be, the fact is that it is an anomaly. The situation could be remedied by conferring on the Parliament the power to cancel a Council directive, on the basis of an absolute majority of its members, for a limited period. In such, admittedly rather unlikely, cases the procedure would require a new proposal to be made by the Commission for the process to be relaunched. This sort of provision would not delay the decision-making process unduly but would ensure that a legislative measure adopted by a decision of the Council would at least have the implicit agreement of a majority in the Parliament.

I referred earlier to the role which the Parliament could play in the election of the President of the Commission. The appointment of the other Members of the Commission and of Judges of the Court of Justice should be subject to approval by the Parliament under a similar procedure to that which is currently used for the appointment of members of the Court of Auditors. It is one which is well known in a number of federal systems and is frequently used, for example, in the United States Senate.

Lastly, if we are to consolidate the authority of the Parliament we must introduce plans to strengthen its powers of investigation, to broaden its right of petition, and perhaps to grant it a right of initiative in legislative matters in cases where the Commission fails to act. These are areas where some action has already been taken, or has at least been considered, notably in the draft treaty known as the Spinelli Report[5].

A Parliament with enhanced powers and prestige is an essential element in a democratic European structure. But democratic aspirations do not stop there. In the Preamble to the Single Act, the concepts of democracy and basic rights appeared for the first time in a basic European legal text. A specific provision on basic rights should be incorporated into the Treaty itself—in Article 4, for example. A proposal along these lines was made by Belgium, but was discarded during the negotiations on the Single Act. Similarly, the Community itself should subscribe to the Strasbourg Convention on Human Rights as well as to certain conventions on social welfare, so that citizens of the Community can identify language guaranteeing their rights in the texts of the Treaties themselves.

Democracy is also—perhaps above all else—the right to vote. Clearly, the European Parliament must be encouraged to develop a uniform procedure for European elections which will enable all the citizens of the Community to participate in them, regardless of their place of residence. This is not the case today.

Finally, I favour granting voting rights in municipal elections to Community citizens provided certain residence requirements are met. There is substantial resistance to this in Belgium, as well as elsewhere, but in the context of Europe's political union, such a development is inevitable.

The 'subsidiarity' Principle

The frequency with which the principle of 'subsidiarity' has come up over the past few months is a measure of the Community's success. Several years ago, the fear was that the Community would stagnate or collapse; today, the fear is that the Community is going too fast. This is a good sign. The fear of centralised power, however, which is reflected

---

[5] Draft Treaty establishing the European Union known as the Spinelli Report (after the late Italian Minister of Foreign Affairs who co-ordinated its preparation). Adopted by the European Parliament on 14 February 1984 (237 votes in favour, 31 against, 43 abstentions).

in the insistence on the principle of 'subsidiarity', is a legitimate concern. It is not unique to the Community: we find evidence of it in the constitutional development in the majority of our Member States and particularly in Belgium's current federalisation process.

It seems reasonable, therefore, to include a provision in the Treaty analogous to the one found in the Spinelli proposal: 'The Union shall only act to carry out those tasks which may be undertaken more effectively in common than by the Member States acting separately, in particular those whose execution requires action by the Union because their dimension or effects extend beyond national frontiers'. (See footnote on page 54).

The provision states a general principle only. It may be necessary to go into greater detail, especially in areas where there is greater sensitivity to national idiosyncrasies—in cultural matters, for example, or certain aspects of social welfare legislation. It might be necessary to specify in greater detail the respective areas of responsibility of the Community and of the Member States in fields such as these.

In view of the emergence of the principle of subsidiarity, treaty provisions will be needed to enable a Member State to have recourse to the Court of Justice if it feels that a Community decision exceeds its area of authority as defined by this principle.

The principle must not, however, be seen purely as a negative factor which enables Member States to defend their rights *vis-à-vis* the Community apparatus. The approach is essentially a rational one which reflects a determination to be both efficient and consistent in identifying those activities which can best be carried out at the Community level and distinguishing them from activities which are best dealt with either under national law or by regional institutions. The people of the Community, for whom all these measures are actually intended, need to be made to feel that there is a rational, coherent basis, at each level, for the approach taken.

Political Unity

The President of the Commission, Jacques Delors, stated recently that political co-operation was not progressing rapidly enough in relation to economic and social integration. I share this point of view. The machinery for political co-operation operates reasonably well, but its limitations have become apparent over the last few months. The rapid pace of events in Eastern Europe, the major role which devolved on the Community following the decision of the Paris Summit of the seven leading industrialised nations to task the Community with the co-ordination of aid initiatives for Poland and Hungary—all of these developments probably mean that a new approach to political co-operation is required. This has to be more flexible, better attuned to Community activity, and based on a joint conviction which can then be translated into Community action.

The need for a joint foreign policy worthy of the name is, in other words, greater than ever. I see no reason why the challenge created by the democratic explosion in Eastern Europe should not be used as a catalyst for this, and as proof that we are, in fact, able to develop a foreign policy of this kind. After all, since the European Council held in Strasbourg, we have repeatedly stated that we, the Community, would be the cornerstone of the future Pan-European construction, of which German reunification would be the first step. From now on we must speak to our East European counterparts, to the major powers, and in fora such as the CSCE with one voice. We shall only be taken seriously if we assert ourselves and make a concrete contribution to the planning and the building of this Pan-European entity. But we have to earn the right to be heard; it cannot be demanded as a right.

Without waiting for institutional reforms in this area, without advocating immediately a formal 'Communitarisation' of the political activity of the Twelve (although that would be my fondest wish), I believe that an operational approach to the questions posed by the liberalisation in Eastern Europe can already be devised. It calls for practical attitudes and behaviour of a kind which can lead to a Community-wide '*Ostpolitik*'.

Foreign Ministers should therefore pool their information and develop principles and guidelines which can provide a common framework for activities undertaken by the Community or under European Political Co-operation or by Member States, *vis-à-vis* the countries of Central and Eastern Europe. The point is that a comprehensive approach is required to see what can be done to encourage political development; to guarantee security; to contribute to the reorganisation and the revitalisation of the economy as well as to the training of new leaders; to foster regional co-operation; and to facilitate integration into a world which is quite different from the one these countries knew 40 years ago. There is no shortage of tasks and aims.

Some of these matters can best be pursued bilaterally. Others can be handled by the private sector or through university contacts and others through the Community or the CSCE process, or by multilateral organisations, such as the Council of Europe. But an overall view is needed. If we intend to be instrumental in setting up the new European architecture, then we have to agree on this overall view and co-ordinate our efforts. If this is to be achieved, Ministers must get into the habit of meeting regularly, both as the Council of the Communities, where decisions based on applications of the Treaties are concerned, and in the context of European Political Co-operation (EPC). The General Affairs Council, whose meetings are often rather dull, must again become the hub of political decision-making for the Community. We do not need more statements but we do need to carry out a meaningful policy.

Ministerial decisions on Treaty matters and on aspects of European Political Co-operation are prepared by ambassadors and political directors respectively. By the same token, it would be logical for them to meet on matters relating to the whole '*Ostpolitik*' field which has now taken on such global importance. The Irish Presidency set the tone for this in an unprecedented way by bringing Ministers of Foreign Affairs together, each flanked by his ambassador and by his political director.

In the same context, in order to bring about the necessary cohesion, we must also see what can be done to improve the way in which the Commission's role is defined. To give this central process of political decision-making the basic infrastructure it needs, we may have to reinforce the Political Co-operation Secretariat, providing it with a specialised Eastern European section and integrating it into the General Secretariat of the Council. The Political Co-operation Secretariat needs to be encouraged to work closely with the services of the Commission in order to make better use of the combined diplomatic expertise and know-how of the Member States. Better results can be obtained without necessarily modifying the present institutional framework.

A common foreign policy can only grow out of political union but this, in turn, is inconceivable if it does not also involve security questions. It is obvious that security issues are at the forefront of discussions on Germany and on the problems of Eastern Europe. If we want the Twelve to continue to play a major role in these discussions, we must be able to discuss security matters freely in the framework of EPC. Despite statements to the contrary, it is not true that the Single Act prevents this major aspect of European stability from being addressed. The following passage from Article 30 of the Single Act makes this quite clear: 'The High Contracting Parties consider that closer co-operation on questions of European security would contribute in an essential way to the development of a European identity in external policy matters'.

Is this not exactly what we are talking about when we speak of our desire to construct the Pan-European community of tomorrow? In practice, all that is required is for us to give the political aspects and the economic aspects of security—which we are obliged to co-ordinate under the Single Act—a direction commensurate with current needs. We must stop seeing these matters as taboo subjects.

Our counterparts in Moscow and in Washington—in Eastern Europe and in the West—fail to understand the artificial distinctions which we maintain between our Community approaches, on the one hand, and Political Co-operation, on the other. There is surely a contradiction between our stated intention of playing a key role in international affairs—or the fact that we are a major economic power—and our apparent inability to regard ourselves as an entity with a global view of foreign relations and an ability to act accordingly. Developments in Eastern Europe call for urgent answers. We do not have time to indulge in visionary speculation. Europe may have been partly built on a vision, but was also constructed under the pressure of events. I hope the shock from developments in Eastern Europe proves as salutary.

The proposals which Belgium has formulated to strengthen the effectiveness and the democratic character of our institutional apparatus, to codify the principle of subsidiarity, and to increase the impact of our external action, make a coherent whole. They were transmitted to our Community partners in the form of an *aide-mémoire* circulated on 20 March 1990. The paper had no legal status and was intended only as a basis for discussion and a contribution to a far-reaching debate on the future of the Community. It is still too early to discuss procedures but what is important is that the governments of the Community should not gloss over the problem.

Belgium has always nurtured high ambitions for the Community and has sought to create a dynamic Europe with the ability to play its part as an independent actor both in Europe and on the world scene. This need not be an obstacle—now or in the future—to the creation of a Pan-European Community in which today's 'European Community' would maintain political, economic or institutional relations with the other European countries, for example within the CSCE. This is a legitimate goal which can no longer be regarded as utopian. That does not make it easy to achieve. It requires vision, perseverance and firmness. The Pan-European structure will have no use for a weakened European Community bereft of ambition. It needs a dynamic and unified Community and our contribution, we hope, is in helping that sort of Community to emerge.

Appendix I

THE BELGIAN MEMORANDUM[1]

Several considerations combine to suggest that the European Community be given a new stimulus towards political union.

(a) Firstly, the transformation of the political scene in Europe is creating a climate of uncertainty and giving rise to speculation. It is time to point out that:
  - the European Community has shown an example of reconciliation and prosperity to the whole continent;
  - this anchor point, far from disintegrating must, in a changing continent, be strengthened and developed in the interests of all Europeans;
  - the Community's political purpose, which has always been present in the European Treaties, now becomes essential for guaranteeing its credibility as a major actor on the European stage.

(b) Secondly, the internal development of the Community, in particular the completion of the internal market and economic and monetary union, highlights the growing 'democratic shortfall' in the current institutional framework and requires reform involving a transfer of political power at Community level and a better definition of the principle of subsidiarity.

(c) Thirdly, the special responsibility which the Community is generally thought to have for seeking solutions to the problems

---

[1] Text of a memorandum forwarded by Minister of Foreign Affairs, Mark Eyskens, on behalf of the Belgian Government, to members of the European Council of Ministers on 20 March 1990.

of Central and Eastern Europe requires a capacity to take effective and consistent external action, at least in that part of the world.

In that situation, it is necessary in the first place to abide by the aims which the Community has already set itself:

- completion of the internal market by adopting the legislative programme in the White Paper between now and the end of 1992; introduction of economic and monetary union in accordance with a plan to be laid down by the Intergovernmental Conference called for the end of 1990;
- development of the Community's social dimension along the lines indicated by the Social Charter adopted in Strasbourg in December 1989.

These aims must be energetically pursued but, for the reasons set out above, should be accompanied by a corresponding effort in the institutional and political fields.

The aim of the proposals which follow is to:

- strengthen the existing institutional machinery, in order to make it more effective:
- increase the democratic component of the institutional machinery, by reinforcing the powers of Parliament and developing the Community's social dimension;
- developing convergence between political co-operation and Community policy; here, the policy towards Central and Eastern Europe could be the first opportunity to put this into practice.

I. *INSTITUTIONAL MACHINERY*

1. *The Council*

In order to make the Council more effective as a decision-making forum, the *qualified majority* should become the rule for all decisions taken in the area covered by the Treaties. If exceptions are unavoidable, they should be very few in number. A preliminary list of the relevant Articles in the Treaties is appended.

Unanimity would still be required to extend the range of subjects over which the Community has jurisdiction (Article 235) and for constitutional provisions (revision of the Treaties, accessions).

2. *The Commission*

   (a) In order to reinforce the Commission's implementing powers it will be necessary to return to the spirit of the Single Act and in practice to restrict as much as possible the requirements for delegation and the specific cases in which the Council reserves the right to exercise power itself (see Article 145—3rd indent).

   (b) In order to increase the Commission's effectiveness as Community executive, it will be necessary to:

   strengthen the role of the President

   The President should be elected by the Parliament by a qualified majority of its component members on the basis of a nomination submitted by the European Council before the other members of the Commission are appointed. It would be understood that the elected President plays a decisive role in allocating responsibilities among the Commissioners. This would no doubt enable him to exert real influence over the selection by Member States of the candidates presented for Commissioners;

   reduce the number of Commissioners (P.M.)

3. *The Court*

   The authority of the Court is beginning to be undermined by the failure of Member States to take the necessary action on certain Judgments. Ways should be sought, and possibly incorporated in the Treaties, to ensure that Judgments are more fully enforced.

II. *DEMOCRATIC SHORTFALL*

1. *The Parliament*

   There is no doubt that the Parliament should become more efficient in operation (in particular in order to cope more effectively with the additional tasks arising from completion of the internal market and from the Single Act), but that is essentially for Parliament itself to decide. The way to reduce the democratic shortfall is not by increasing efficiency but by increasing the powers of the Parliament, mainly in the legislative sphere (although changes might also be considered in the budgetary sphere).

The Parliament's main demand is for a *share in decision-making*. The following reforms would entail a form of joint decision-making:

- extending the *co-operation procedure* to all legislative decisions taken by the Council by a qualified majority (e.g. Articles 63 and 75);
- stipulating that legislative decisions (adopted by the Council on a second reading on completion of the co-operation procedure) may be annulled within three months of their adoption if Parliament votes by an absolute majority of its component members. In this case the procedure should be begun again with a new Commission proposal.

This would do away with one of the main criticisms of the current practice, which enables the Council to adopt on a second reading Directives which are contrary to the wishes of a majority in the Parliament. Henceforth, every legislative provision would therefore presuppose a Council decision and at least tacit agreement by a majority in the Parliament;

- extending the consent procedure to amendments to the Treaty (Article 236), to own resources (Article 201) and important international agreements (extension of Article 238) and to the uniform procedure for elections to the European Parliament (Article 138(3)).
- conferring on the Parliament the responsibility for electing the President of the Commission (see above). The other members of the Commission (and the judges of the Court of Justice) would continue to be appointed by the Member States but would be subject to a Parliamentary approval procedure (as the members of the Court of Auditors are now).

Amendments of less importance might also be considered:

- strengthening the powers of committees of inquiry

- right of petition in Parliament
- right to take the legislative initiative where the Commission fails to act.

2. *A People's Europe/Human Rights*

It will be difficult to achieve a People's Europe, which is directly linked with free movement of persons in the context of the single market, without introducing the qualified majority (see above and Annex).

To strengthen the democratic nature of the institutional apparatus, it would be desirable for a provision on human rights to be written in to the Treaty and for the Community as such to accede to the Strasbourg Convention on Human Rights and to certain agreements relating to social rights.

The Parliament should be encouraged to draw up a uniform procedure for the European elections: this would also enable all Community citizens living in the Community to take part in the elections whatever their nationality.

Subject to certain residence conditions, the right to vote in local elections, which has been included in a proposal for a Directive, should be phased in for Community citizens throughout Community territory.

III. *SUBSIDIARITY*

At a time when the development of the European enterprise is leading to a major transfer of legislative power at Community level, it is essential that the principle of subsidiarity be formally written into the Treaty, for example in the form in which it was expressed in the draft Spinelli Treaty: 'The Union shall only act to carry out those tasks which may be undertaken more effectively in common than by the Member States acting separately, in particular those whose execution requires action by the Union because their dimension or effects extend beyond national frontiers.'

This broad provision should be supplemented by more precise details of respective powers in sensitive areas in which national traditions frequently differ.

Since the principle of subsidiarity is an ongoing concept, the provisions of the Treaty should so be formulated as to enable a Member State to appeal to the Court of Justice if it considers that a Community decision exceeds the Community's powers as defined by the principle.

IV. POLITICAL CO-OPERATION

The political challenge constituted by developments in Eastern Europe has shown up more clearly the limitations of the existing machinery of political co-operation. The new international context calls more than ever for truly joint foreign policy. If it is true that the Twelve regard themselves as a focal point for future Pan-European integration, the only logical course of action is for them to take part in the discussions as a political entity. This applies not only to a common '*Ostpolitik*', but also to new relations with the great powers and also when taking up a position in international bodies such as the Council of Europe or the CSCE. We will be taken seriously only insofar as we assert ourselves. A share in the major decisions of the time has to be earned.

Since answers are now expected without any more delay, there can be no question at this stage of spending time on a hasty revision of Article 30 of the Single Act. It must be hoped, however, that the constraints forced on us by events will encourage us in the not too distant future to amend rules which no longer meet the requirements of the action which it is our ambition and duty to take. In the meantime, in view of the special situation which has been brought about by liberalisation in the East, the Twelve must at least adopt a practical attitude and pragmatic approach to problems awaiting a solution. This might take the following form:

1. The Ministers for Foreign Affairs should work together to define and organise a set of principles and guidelines for political co-operation and co-operation by the Member States in relation to Eastern and Central European countries which would serve as a common framework for the activities of the Communities. To be consistent, the framework must cover all aspects: economic and political, bilateral and multilateral (CSCE). For this purpose the

Ministers should adopt the custom of meeting regularly, both in the Council and in political co-operation. The General Affairs Council should once again become the Community's political decision-making centre. It must endeavour to pursue a policy rather than produce endless declarations. Similarly, it is conceivable that COREPER and the Political Directors (Political Co-operation) might together prepare the decisions on which would be based a global approach to the questions arising out of developments in Central and Eastern Europe and that the role of the Commission should be better defined, so as to secure the desired consistency.

2. It might also be desirable to obtain a better mix between expertise and diplomatic information from the Member States and the Commission's experience. Without changing the institutional framework and with due regard for the respective powers of each party, it would be possible to conduct an initial experiment in synergy by setting up a 'specialised task force' made up of some diplomats specialising in Eastern European countries, who would be seconded by the Member States, and by some Commission officials. This nucleus would serve as a centre for analysis, study and co-ordination on Eastern Europe to the benefit of both the Council and the Commission.

3. With a view to political union and, more particularly, to actual participation in the discussions which are about to take place in the CSCE, it is both desirable and necessary that it should be possible to discuss security issues in the broadest sense without restriction in political co-operation. Without prejudice to the powers of other institutions, which are themselves destined to change, the Member States have no cause to deprive themselves everlastingly of the opportunity to discuss this essential aspect among themselves.

FINAL REMARKS

1. From a procedural point of view, the European Council might decide:

- either to call a special Intergovernmental Conference;
- or to entrust the dossier to the Intergovernmental Conference called by the Strasbourg European Council.

There are advantages and disadvantages to both solutions and in practice the difference between the two options does not seem very significant, as long as the timing is the same.

2. The aim of these proposals is to bring the Community nearer to political union. They therefore tend to favour an 'intensive Europe'. They do not constitute a barrier to the building of an 'extensive Europe' within which the Community and its Member States would maintain political, economic and institutional relations of another type with other European countries.

Sectors now subject to unanimity to which the qualified majority rule might be applied.

1. *Internal market* : Article 100a(2) lays down *three exceptions* to the qualified majority rule.
    1.1 *Fiscal provisions* : it is conceivable that major fiscal decisions (for example on levels of taxation) could be taken unanimously, but that decisions relating to the basis of assessment and the methods of taxation could be taken by a qualified majority.
    1.2 *Free movement of persons* : the qualified majority rule should be introduced along with a declaration (similar to the one in the Single Act) reserving the right of the Member States to act (and their duty to co-operate) in matters relating to immigration and measures to combat terrorism and crime.
    1.3 *Rights and interests of employed persons* : the right to act by a qualified majority on social questions is one of the European Parliament's main demands; it might be accompanied by a precise definition of the principle of subsidiarity in this sector.
2. *Research* : Article 130q lays down *two exceptions* to the qualified majority rule; establishment of the framework programme and the setting up of joint undertakings. These two exceptions ought to be abolished. The qualified majority and co-operation with the Parliament could also be introduced for Euratom research programmes (Article 7 of Euratom Treaty).
3. *Environment* : Article 130s lays down *unanimity* as the rule: the rule should become the qualified majority.

4. *Coal and Steel* : introduce into the ECSC Treaty a provision corresponding to Article 113 of the EEC Treaty so that matters of common commercial policy in the coal and steel sector cease to be subject to unanimity.

Appendix 2

LONDON DECLARATION ON A TRANSFORMED NORTH ATLANTIC ALLIANCE

Issued by the Heads of State and Government participating in the meeting of the North Atlantic Council in London on 5-6 July 1990

1. Europe has entered a new, promising era. Central and Eastern Europe is liberating itself. The Soviet Union has embarked on the long journey toward a free society. The walls that once confined people and ideas are collapsing. Europeans are determining their own destiny. They are choosing freedom. They are choosing economic liberty. They are choosing peace. They are choosing a Europe whole and free. As a consequence, this Alliance must and will adapt.

2. The North Atlantic Alliance has been the most successful defensive alliance in history. As our Alliance enters its fifth decade and looks ahead to a new century, it must continue to provide for the common defence. This Alliance has done much to bring about the new Europe. No-one, however, can be certain of the future. We need to keep standing together, to extend the long peace we have enjoyed these past four decades. Yet our Alliance must be even more an agent of change. It can help build the structures of a more united continent, supporting security and stability with the strength of our shared faith in democracy, the rights of the individual, and the peaceful resolution of disputes. We reaffirm that security and stability do not lie solely in the military dimension, and we intend to enhance the political component of our Alliance as provided for by Article 2 of our Treaty.

3. The unification of Germany means that the division of Europe is also being overcome. A united Germany in the Atlantic Alliance of free

democracies and part of the growing political and economic integration of the European Community will be an indispensable factor of stability, which is needed in the heart of Europe. The move within the European Community towards political union, including the development of a European identity in the domain of security, will also contribute to Atlantic solidarity and to the establishment of a just and lasting order of peace throughout the whole of Europe.

4. We recognise that, in the new Europe, the security of every state is inseparably linked to the security of its neighbours. NATO must become an institution where Europeans, Canadians and Americans work together not only for the common defence, but to build new partnerships with all the nations of Europe. The Atlantic Community must reach out to the countries of the East which were our adversaries in the Cold War, and extend to them the hand of friendship.

5. We will remain a defensive alliance and will continue to defend all the territory of all of our members. We have no aggressive intentions and we commit ourselves to the peaceful resolution of all disputes. We will never in any circumstance be the first to use force.

6. The member states of the North Atlantic Alliance propose to the member states of the Warsaw Treaty Organisation a joint declaration in which we solemnly state that we are no longer adversaries and reaffirm our intention to refrain from the threat or use of force against the territorial integrity or political independence of any state, or from acting in any other manner inconsistent with the purposes and principles of the United Nations Charter and with the CSCE Final Act. We invite all other CSCE member states to join us in this commitment to non-aggression.

7. In that spirit, and to reflect the changing political role of the Alliance, we today invite President Gorbachev on behalf of the Soviet Union, and representatives of the other Central and Eastern European countries to come to Brussels and address the North Atlantic Council. We today also invite the governments of the Union of Soviet Socialist Republics, the Czech and Slovak Federal Republic, the Hungarian Republic, the Republic of Poland, the People's Republic of Bulgaria and Romania to come to NATO, not just to visit, but to establish regular diplomatic liaison with NATO. This will make it possible for

us to share with them our thinking and deliberations in this historic period of change.

8. Our Alliance will do its share to overcome the legacy of decades of suspicion. We are ready to intensify military contacts, including those of NATO Military Commanders, with Moscow and other Central and Eastern European capitals.

9. We welcome the invitation to NATO Secretary General Manfred Wörner to visit Moscow and meet with Soviet leaders.

10. Military leaders from throughout Europe gathered earlier this year in Vienna to talk about their forces and doctrine. NATO proposes another such meeting this Autumn to promote common understanding. We intend to establish an entirely different quality of openness in Europe, including an agreement on 'Open Skies'.

11. The significant presence of North American conventional and US nuclear forces in Europe demonstrates the underlying political compact that binds North America's fate to Europe's democracies. But, as Europe changes, we must profoundly alter the way we think about defence.

12. To reduce our military requirements, sound arms control agreements are essential. That is why we put the highest priority on completing this year the first treaty to reduce and limit conventional armed forces in Europe (CFE) along with the completion of a meaningful CSBM package. These talks should remain in continuous session until the work is done. Yet we hope to go further. We propose that, once a CFE Treaty is signed, follow-on talks should begin with the same membership and mandate, with the goal of building on the current agreement with additional measures, including measures to limit manpower in Europe. With this goal in mind, a commitment will be given at the time of signature of the CFE Treaty concerning the manpower levels of a unified Germany.

13. Our objective will be to conclude the negotiations on the follow-on to CFE and CSBMs as soon as possible and looking to the follow-up meeting of the CSCE to be held in Helsinki in 1992. We will seek through new conventional arms control negotiations, within the CSCE framework, further far-reaching measures in the 1990s to limit the offensive capability of conventional armed forces in Europe, so as to prevent any nation from maintaining disproportionate military

power on the continent. NATO's High Level Task Force will formulate a detailed position for these follow-on conventional arms control talks. We will make provisions as needed for different regions to redress disparities and to ensure that no one's security is harmed at any stage. Furthermore, we will continue to explore broader arms control and confidence-building opportunities. This is an ambitious agenda, but it matches our goal: enduring peace in Europe.

14. As Soviet troops leave Eastern Europe and a treaty limiting conventional armed forces is implemented, the Alliance's integrated force structure and its strategy will change fundamentally to include the following elements:

- NATO will field smaller and restructured active forces. These forces will be highly mobile and versatile so that Allied leaders will have maximum flexibility in deciding how to respond to a crisis. It will rely increasingly on multinational corps made up of national units.
- NATO will scale back the readiness of its active units, reducing training requirements and the number of exercises.
- NATO will rely more heavily on the ability to build up larger forces if and when they might be needed.

15. To keep the peace, the Alliance must maintain for the foreseeable future an appropriate mix of nuclear and conventional forces, based in Europe, and kept up to date where necessary. But, as a defensive Alliance, NATO has always stressed that none of its weapons will ever be used except in self-defence and that we seek the lowest and most stable level of nuclear forces needed to secure the prevention of war.

16. The political and military changes in Europe, and the prospects of further changes, now allow the Allies concerned to go further. They will thus modify the size and adapt the tasks of their nuclear deterrent forces. They have concluded that, as a result of the new political and military conditions in Europe, there will be a significantly reduced role for sub-strategic nuclear systems of the shortest range. They have decided specifically that, once negotiations begin on short-range nuclear forces, the Alliance will propose, in return for reciprocal action by the Soviet Union, the elimination of all its nuclear artillery shells from Europe.

17. New negotiations between the United States and the Soviet Union on the reduction of short-range nuclear forces should begin shortly after a CFE agreement is signed. The Allies concerned will develop an arms control framework for these negotiations which takes into account our requirements for far fewer nuclear weapons, and the diminished need for sub-strategic nuclear systems of the shortest range.

18. Finally, with the total withdrawal of Soviet stationed forces and the implementation of a CFE agreement, the Allies concerned can reduce their reliance on nuclear weapons. These will continue to fulfil an essential role in the overall strategy of the Alliance to prevent war by ensuring that there are no circumstances in which nuclear retaliation in response to military action might be discounted. However, in the transformed Europe, they will be able to adopt a new NATO strategy making nuclear forces truly weapons of last resort.

19. We approve the mandate given in Turnberry to the North Atlantic Council in Permanent Session to oversee the ongoing work on the adaptation of the Alliance to the new circumstances. It should report its conclusions as soon as possible.

20. In the context of these revised plans for defence and arms control, and with the advice of NATO Military Authorities and all member states concerned, NATO will prepare a new Allied military strategy moving away from 'forward defence', where appropriate, towards a reduced forward presence and modifying 'flexible response' to reflect a reduced reliance on nuclear weapons. In that connection, NATO will elaborate new force plans consistent with the revolutionary changes in Europe. NATO will also provide a forum for Allied consultation on the upcoming negotiations on short-range nuclear forces.

21. The Conference on Security and Co-operation in Europe (CSCE) should become more prominent in Europe's future, bringing together the countries of Europe and North America. We support a CSCE Summit later this year in Paris which would include the signature of a CFE agreement and would set new standards for the establishment, and preservation, of free societies. It should endorse, inter alia:

- CSCE principles on the right to free and fair elections;
- CSCE commitments to respect and uphold the rule of law;
- CSCE guidelines for enhancing economic co-operation, based on the development of free and competitive market economies; and
- CSCE co-operation on environmental protection.

22. We further propose that the CSCE Summit in Paris decide how the CSCE can be institutionalised to provide a forum for wider political dialogue in a more united Europe. We recommend that CSCE governments establish:

- a programme for regular consultations among member governments at the Heads of State and Government or Ministerial level, at least once each year, with other periodic meetings of officials to prepare for and follow up on these consultations;
- a schedule of CSCE review conferences once every two years to assess progress toward a Europe whole and free;
- a small CSCE secretariat to co-ordinate these meetings and conferences;
- a CSCE mechanism to monitor elections in all the CSCE countries, on the basis of the Copenhagen Document;
- a CSCE Centre for the Prevention of Conflict that might serve as a forum for exchanges of military information, discussion of unusual military activities, and the conciliation of disputes involving CSCE member states; and
- a CSCE parliamentary body, the Assembly of Europe, to be based on the existing parliamentary assembly of the Council of Europe, in Strasbourg, and include representatives of all CSCE member states.

The sites of these new institutions should reflect the fact that the newly democratic countries of Central and Eastern Europe form part of the political structures of the new Europe.

23. Today, our Alliance begins a major transformation. Working with all the countries of Europe, we are determined to create enduring peace on this continent.

Index

Aron, Raymond 8

Baker, James 37
Belgium 31, 52, 54, 58
   Federalisation of 55
   and the Institute for the Study of Peace and Security 32
   Memorandum of Government of 58–9, 60–8
BENELUX countries 26
Berlin, revolt in (1953) 3
Berlin Wall 10
Brezhnev doctrine 6
   renunciation of by Gorbachev 3, 14
   see also Gorbachev, Mikhail
Bulgaria, political reform in 3, 42–3

Canada 30
Capitalism 4, 11, 28
China, People's Republic of 14
Cold War 1, 31
   end of 4, 11, 16, 34
Communism 1
   'implosion' of 9–11
   maintenance of 8
   see also Marxism, Marxism–Leninism
Conference for Security and Co-operation in Europe 10, 30, 56, 57, 59
   Final Act of (Helsinki) 31, 35, 37
   Baskets I & II of 36
   Basket III of 10
   see also Helsinki process

Conventional Forces in Europe (CFE) negotiations 30, 32–3, 36, 39, 41
Council for Mutual Economic Assistance (COMECON) 40
Czechoslovakia 23
   invasion of (1968) 3, 6, 10
   political reform in 3, 15, 27, 42–3

Delors, Jacques 55
   Report of Inter-governmental Conference of 47
Democracy 10, 19, 31
   challenges for in West 11–13
   in EEC 52–4
   in Russia 8
Détente 10, 23, 27, 31, 35, 36, 41, 42

European Bank for Development and Reconstruction 18
European (Economic) Community (EC/EEC) 2, 16
   aid to Eastern Bloc, role of in 17–19
   aid to 'Third World' of 40–1
   Commission of 17, 46, 50, 52, 53, 57
   President of 51, 53
   Council of Ministers of 50, 51, 52, 53
   Court of Auditors of 53
   Economic and Monetary Union of 29, 37, 43, 46–7, 49, 52
   and European confederation 31, 40
   European Court of Justice of 37, 52, 53, 55
   General Affairs Council of 57

and German reunification   25
  see also Germany, reunification of
joint foreign policy of   17–18, 22–3,
  55–9
Parliament of   33, 37, 41, 43, 50, 51
  legislative powers of   52–4
Political Co-operation Secretariat of
  57
Political union of   22–4, 37, 39, 43,
  48
Single Act of   22, 26, 46, 50–1, 52,
  57, 58
  Preamble to   54
and the Soviet Union   31, 39
Treaty of Rome establishing   26, 39,
  50–1, 52, 53, 55, 57
European Free Trade Association
  (EFTA)   37–9, 40
European integration   2–3, 16, 17, 19,
  24, 37, 48
European Steel and Coal Community
  2, 47

First World War   1, 28
France   3, 26, 29
  nuclear forces of   34
Fukuyama, Francis   11

German Democratic Republic (GDR),
  Christian Democratic Union of
  27
  Liberal Party of   27
  political reform in   3, 25, 27, 28,
  42–3
Germany   3
  reunification of   24–9, 30, 36, 37, 40,
  56
Germany, Federal Republic of   17
  and the EEC   25
  and NATO   27
  and nuclear weapons   32
  Ostpolitik of   26, 43
Glasnost   3, 14
Gorbachev, Mikhail   3, 19
  and German reunification   29
    see also Germany, reunification of
  and Marxism–Leninism   6

and nationality problem   4
reforms of   7, 13–15, 21, 33, 43
Gulag Archipelago   3

Harmel doctrine   10, 34–5
Helsinki (CSCE) process   10, 17, 24,
  25, 30
Hungary   23
  Invasion of (1956)   3, 6, 10
  political reform in   3, 15, 27
  Western aid to   18, 56

Japan   5, 37

Kerensky, Aleksandr   8
Khrushchev, Nikita   4
Kohl, Helmut   26, 27, 40

Lome Agreement   41

Market economy   6, 11–12, 18, 31–2
  competition in   20–1
  and democracy   19–21
  see also Democracy
Marxism   1, 8
  and capitalism   4
  ideological failure of   5–6
Marxism–Leninism   1, 3
  renunciation of   4, 6
Marx, Karl   5
Mitterrand, François   40
Monnett, Jean   26

Nomenklatura   5, 7
North Atlantic Treaty Organisation
  (NATO)   10, 16, 23, 24, 30, 31,
  33, 35, 36
  and German reunification   25, 26,
  28, 29
    see also Germany, reunification of
  North Atlantic Council of, London
  Declaration of (1990)   69–74
  and the Soviet Union   31
Nuclear deterrence   33–4

INDEX

October Revolution (1917) 1, 8
Oder-Neisse Line 30, 36
'Open Skies' 30
Organisation for European Co-operation and Development 17

Paris Summit 56
Perestroika 3, 6, 14, 43
Poland 23, 30
  General Jaruzelski's coup in (1981) 3
  political reform in 3, 27
  Western aid to 18, 56

Romania, overthrow of Ceausescu in 8, 15
  political reform in 3, 42–3

Second World War 1, 2, 3, 6, 8, 10–11, 25, 31
Soviet Union 24, 37
  communism in 8–9
    see also Communism
  Communist Party of 4
    monopoly status of 21–2
  economy of 4, 5, 6
  and German reunification 28
    see also Germany, reunification of
  Western aid to 18
Spaak, Paul Henri 33, 47
Spinelli Report 54, 55
Sputnik 9

De Standaard 40
Stalin, Josef 6, 33
Strasbourg Convention on Human Rights 54
Strategic Arms Reduction Talks (START) 30, 32
'Subsidiarity' 50, 54–5, 58

Third Industrial Revolution 10
Toynbee, Arnold 49

United Kingdom 26
  nuclear forces of 34
United Nations Economic Commission for Europe 36
United States of America 26, 29, 30, 34
  and European integration 37, 39
  Senate of 53

Vertragsemeinschaft 27

Warsaw Pact 10, 16, 23, 30, 31, 32, 35, 36
  and German reunification 25, 26
    see also Germany, reunification of
Western European Union (WEU) 23, 47

Yalto Conference (1945) 3